COWBOY SONGS OLD & NEW

Gary Coover
&
Pipp Gillette

Rollston Press

CowboySongs Old & New
by Gary Coover & Pipp Gillette

Copyright © 2020 Rollston Press

ISBN-13: 978-1-7326121-5-0

ISBN-10: 1-7326121-5-3

All titles are traditional or public domain unless noted otherwise.

Also from Rollston Press: *Cowboy Concertina* (2018)

Front Cover: *Concertina at the Campfire* by William Matthews (2018). Great Basin Studio, 2540 Walnut St, Denver, Colorado 80205. (www.williammatthewsstudio.com)

Back Cover: Excerpt of painting by George Martin Ottinger, *Away Away to the Mountain Dell: The Valley of the Free Immigrant Train* (1897), oil on canvas, 20 x 40 in. (50.8 x 101.6 cm), Courtesy of the Springville Museum of Art, Springville, Utah. (www.smofa.org)

Rollston Press

1717 Ala Wai Blvd, Suite 1703
Honolulu, HI 96815
USA

www.rollstonpress.com
info@rollstonpress.com

TABLE OF CONTENTS

Troubadour

Waddie Mitchell

HE CALLS HIMSELF A SONGSTER
THAT LOVES THE TUNE AND LORE
THAT HELPS REVIVE AND KEEP ALIVE
SOME MUSIC LOVED BEFORE
SEARCHES, ROOTS, AND WEARS OUT BOOTS
THAT PROPPED THE NEAR CLOSED DOORS
THE OLD DAYS CALL HIM MINSTREL
WE, A COWBOY TROUBADOR

He knows the music's reasons
And its artists and its feel
He puts to test and puts to rest
All doubt if it is real

And transports us to vistas
He has painted for our minds
Rides nerves of raw emotion
Through the rapids of their times

Shares histories and mysteries
Long nights and good bronc rides
Changing times and changing minds
Realities and lies

Reminds us we are human
With our flaws and dreams and fears
Aggravates them all with ballads
That still move a soul to tears

He'll yodel then he'll lull ya
Then he'll protest then he'll praise
Plant notes like seeds of melodies
That haunt the mind for days

He makes us feel and helps us heal
Gives insights to the rhymes
That glimpse the old perspectives
From these new and different times

HOWDY

For over 150 years the songs of the cowboys of the American West have charmed and captivated performers and audiences worldwide with tales of cattle drives and bucking broncos, songs of outlaws and greenhorns, and laments of lonesome cowboys and lost loves.

Many of these songs began their life as poems crafted by working cowboys during the long workdays on the trail or back at the ranch in the late evenings. But cowboy poetry is not just for "edumacated" folks – it is a heartfelt expression of the cowboy life that often derives from old British Isles ballads, Victorian verse, songs of sailormen and lumberjacks, dime novel adventures, newspaper headlines, local folklore, and real-life experiences both good and bad.

The songs in this book are predominantly traditional and in the public domain and are mostly from the late 1800's. There are a few newer songs included, as there should be, since the cowboy's work and lifestyle continue in many places today. We've also included a vaquero song from Mexico, a stockman song from Down Under and a paniolo song from the Big Island of Hawaii. The Hollywood movie cowboy songs of the 1930's and 1940's are from a much different era, and anyway, trying to round up all those copyright permissions would have been trickier than calming a stampede of panicked longhorns.

It has been a real treat to collaborate on this book with cowboy singer and storyteller Pipp Gillette from Crockett, Texas. The Gillette Brothers are some of the finest interpreters and performers of authentic cowboy music today and many of the songs in this book come from their recordings. Pipp often teams up with renowned cowboy poet Waddie Mitchell and it is a great honor to be able to include some of their collaborations.

If you are a guitar player, every song includes full lyrics and basic guitar chord symbols, and most of the music is shown in the same key as the recordings. If you happen to be a concertina player, *Cowboy Concertina* (2018) has all the same songs specifically arranged for the Anglo concertina.

So, pack away your six-shooter, hitch up your horse, finish your chores, pour yourself an ice-cold sarsaparilla, tip back your hat and set a spell while you enjoy singing these poetic and historical songs of the great American West.

Gary Coover
Rollston Press

INTRODUCTION

The years after the War Between the States marked the beginning of the great trail drive era lasting approximately 30 years. It was also a period of a great migration. People were leaving behind their old lives to start anew in this undefined, new world - The West.

Thrown together where ability outweighed normal old-world conventions, people played and worked together sharing their songs and stories which often took on new life as lyrics were revised to reflect their new experiences.

This period - the end of slavery and the great migration from the British Isles, in particular - is the classic American musical melting pot moment which has fascinated me for years.

I hope you enjoy *Cowboy Songs Old & New*.

Pipp Gillette
Crockett, Texas

Photo by Kevin Martini-Fuller

PERFORMANCE

You can play these songs in a variety of different ways by keeping in mind the many different locations and audiences – in a concert hall, a kitchen, the back forty, in camp, or even to soothe restless livestock.

If you are playing with other musicians, listen closely and strive to enhance and complement the playing of others.

Many of these songs have been handed down from father to son (and mother to daughter) until the handle has fallen off, so you will likely encounter many variations in the melodies and the words. That's perfectly ok, part of the time-honored folk process. As any good cowboy would do, take what you have and know and adapt and rework as you see fit 'til it works for you.

But the most important thing to remember is to keep that wonderful spirit of the Old West alive however you play it, and you'll be following the footsteps and hoofprints of all who have blazed the trail before you.

Songs

AFTER THE CHORES

Pipp Gillette

Gillette Brothers *"Many Long Miles to Ride"* 2006

AIN'T NO MORE CANE ON THE BRAZOS

There ain't no more cane on the Brazos
OH OH OH
They done ground it all in molasses
OH OH OH

You oughta been on the river in nineteen and ten
They drivin' the women like they drive the men

Now Captain don't you do me like you done poor Shine
You drove that bully 'til he went stone blind

Go down old Hannah don't you rise no more
Don't you rise up 'til it's judgement day for sure

There's some in the building and there's some on the farm
There's some in the graveyard and some goin' home

There ain't no more cane on the Brazos
They done ground it all in molasses

Gillette Brothers *"Leaving Cheyenne"* 2012

There ain't no more cane on the Bra - zos. OH OH OH. They

done ground it all in mo - las - ses. OH OH OH.

AT THE END OF THE SANTA FE TRAIL

Bernard Wrigley (1997)

Woollens and cottons of every shade
Buttons and combs going to use them to trade
We've got needles and shears, razors and knives
Hope we won't need them to fight for our lives
Ribbons and earrings and fine velveteens
Bacon and coffee and I hope you like beans
For the trail boss says so
Wait for your first taste of wild buffalo

WE'RE A FLEET OF FINE SHIPS SETTING SAIL
ON A JOURNEY WE KNOW WE DAREN'T FAIL
AND WE HOPE TO FIND OUR HOLY GRAIL
AT THE END OF THE SANTA FE TRAIL

Selling up shop well he must be a fool
Heading out west with your faith in a mule
Don't you know there'll be drought, desert and storm
You'll spend one day roasting and the next keeping warm
Leaving Missouri these words in my ears
The heat and the cold were the least of our fears
For we spent half the time with our eyes in our backs
Shielding the wagons from Indian attacks

Snaked across the prairie, wagon lines of four
Following the ruts that had all been made before
There were times of good health, times we got ill
If the Indians don't get you the Mexicans will
We reached Pawnee Rock on the fourth of July
There I carved my name 'neath the blue prairie sky
And I thought to myself I'm in good company
For Custer's and Kit Carson's names I could see

Leaving Fort Dodge there's a choice we'd to make
A safer mountain route or the short cut to take
For there's no water there you'd turn back if you could
And you'll know what drives men to drink buffalo blood
Head down and onward trying to ignore the heat
Burning your shoulders and blistering feet
When I forced my head up as the sky filled with cries
And there was Fort Union we could trade for supplies

Ninety-two days nearly over at last
Now we're through the far end of the Marietta Pass
And you'd swear there were shots as those whips cracked away
How we cheered those last miles till we reached Santa Fe
End of the trail and I stink like a skunk
Gonna get me a bath and then get me blind drunk
But there's tears in my eyes and my words seem to fail
Now we're here at the end of the Santa Fe Trail

Bernard Wrigley

Verse

Wool-lens and cot-tons of ev-er-y shade, but-tons and combs going to use them for trade. We've got

nee-dles and shears, ra-zors and knives, hope we won't need them to fight for our lives.

Rib-bons and ear-rings and fine vel-ve-teens, ba-con and cof-fee and I hope you like beans. For the

trail boss says so, wait for your first taste of wild buf-falo. WE'RE A

Chorus

FLEET OF FINE SHIPS SET-TING SAIL, ON A JOUR-NEY WE KNOW WE DAREN'T FAIL. AND WE

HOPE TO FIND OUR HO-LY GRAIL, AT THE END OF THE SAN-TA FE TRAIL.

THE BALLAD OF JESSE JAMES

Jesse James was a lad
That killed many a man
He robbed the Danville train
But that dirty little coward
Who shot Mr. Howard
Has laid poor Jesse in his grave

Poor Jesse had a wife
To mourn for his life
Three children they were brave
But the dirty little coward
Who shot Mr. Howard
Has laid poor Jesse in his grave

Now Jesse was a man
A friend to the poor
He never would see a man suffer pain
And with his brother Frank
He robbed the Chicago bank
He stopped the Glendale train

It was Wednesday night
The moon was shining bright
They robbed the Glendale train
The people they did say
For many miles away
It was robbed by Frank and Jesse James

It was with his brother Frank
They robbed the Gallatin bank
And carried the money from the town
It was in this very place
That they had a little race
They shot Captain Sheets to the ground

They went to the crossing
Not very far from there
And there they did the same
With the agent on his knees
He delivered up the keys
To the outlaws, Frank and Jesse James

It was Saturday night
Jesse was at home
Talking with his family brave
Robert Ford came along
Like a thief in the night
And laid poor Jesse in his grave

It was Robert Ford
That dirty little coward
I wonder how he did feel
For he ate of Jesse's bread
And slept in Jesse's bed
Then laid poor Jesse in his grave

Now the people held their breath
When they heard of Jesse's death
Wondered how he came to die
It was one of the gang
Called little Robert Ford
He shot poor Jesse on the sly

Jesse went to his rest
With his hand on his breast
And the devil will surely be on his knee
He was born one day
In the County of Clay
And came from a solitary race

This song was made
By Billy Gashade
As soon as the news did arrive
He said there was no man
With the law in his hand
Who could take Jesse James while alive

Jesse James was a lad
That killed many a man
He robbed the Danville train
But that dirty little coward
Who shot Mr. Howard
Has laid poor Jesse in his grave

Michael Martin Murphey "Cowboy Songs III – Rhymes of the Renegades" 1993

Jes-se James was a lad that killed many a man, he robbed the Dan-ville train.   But that

dir-ty lit-tle cow-ard who shot Mis-ter How-ard, has laid poor Jes-se in his grave.   Poor

Jes-se had a wife   to mourn for his life,   three chil-dren they were   brave.   But the

dir-ty lit-tle cow-ard who shot Mis-ter How-ard, has laid poor Jes-se in his grave.

BEEN ALL AROUND THIS WORLD

Additional cowboy lyrics by Pipp & Guy Gillette

Well the cattle drives are over
And the cars are on the track
The cattle drives are over boys
And the cars are on the track
My doney gal has left me
And she won't be comin' back
Been all around this world

HANG ME, HANG ME
I'LL BE DEAD AND GONE
HANG ME, HANG ME
I'LL BE DEAD AND GONE
IT'S NOT THE HANGING THAT I MIND
IT'S LAYIN' IN THE JAIL SO LONG
BEEN ALL AROUND THIS WORLD

Out on the Davis Mountains
It's there I'll take my stand
Out on the Davis Mountains
There I'll take my stand
My rifle on my shoulder
Six-shooter in my hand
Been all around this world

I had me a big gray horse
Wiggin was his name
Had me a big gray horse
Wiggin was his name
They caught me makin' liquor
I had to leave that claim
Well I've been all around this world

Well the officers arrested me
Put me in the jail
Officers arrested me
And took me down to jail
They said to me young fellow
For you there'll be no bail
Well I've been all around this world

Well mama and papa
Little sister made three
Mama and papa
Little sister made three
They all come to see me
Just hangin' from a gallows tree
Well I've been all around this world

(last time)
HANG ME, HANG ME
I'LL BE DEAD AND GONE
HANG ME, HANG ME
I'LL BE DEAD AND GONE
IT'S NOT THE HANGING THAT I MIND
IT'S LAYIN' IN THE GRAVE SO LONG
BEEN ALL AROUND THIS WORLD

Gillette Brothers "Cowboys, Minstrels and Medicine Shows" 2010

Verse & Chorus

Well the cat-tle drives are o-ver and the cars are on the track.
HANG ME, HANG ME, I'LL BE DEAD AND GONE.

Cat-tle drives are o-ver boys, and the cars are on the track. My
HANG ME, HANG ME, I'LL BE DEAD AND GONE. IT'S

do-ney gal has left me, and she won't be co-ming back.
NOT THE HANG-ING THAT I MIND IT'S LAYIN' IN JAIL SO LONG.

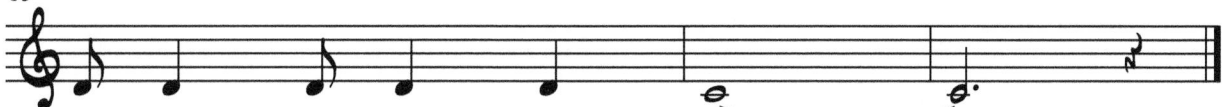

Been all a-round this world.
BEEN ALL A-ROUND THIS WORLD.

BILLY THE KID

I'll sing you a true song of Billy the Kid
I'll sing of the desperate deeds that he did
Out in New Mexico long long ago
When a man's only chance was his own forty-four

When Billy the Kid was a very young lad
In old Silver City he went to the bad
Way out in the West with a gun in his hand
At the age of twelve years he killed his first man

Fair Mexican maidens play guitars and sing
A song about Billy, their boy bandit king
Who 'ere his young manhood had reached his sad end
Had a notch on his pistol for twenty-one men

'Twas on the same night when poor Billy died
He said to his friends I'm not satisfied
There's twenty-one men I have put bullets through
Sheriff Pat Garrett must make twenty-two

Now this is how Billy the Kid met his fate
The bright moon was shinin', the hour was late
Shot down by Pat Garrett who once was his friend
The young outlaw's life had now come to its end

There's many a man with a face fine and fair
Who starts out in life with a chance to be square
Just like poor Billy he wanders astray
And loses his life in the very same way

I'll sing you a true song of Bil - ly the Kid. I'll

sing of the des - per - ate deeds that he did.

Out in New Mex - i - co long long a - go, when a

man's on - ly chance was his own for - ty - four.

BILLY VANERO

Billy Vanero heard them say
In an Arizona town one day
That a band of Apache Indians
Were on the trail of death
Heard them tell of murder done
Three men killed at Rocky Run
They're in danger at the cow ranch
Said Vanero under his breath

The cow ranch forty miles away
Was a little place that lay
In a deep and shady valley
In the mighty wilderness
Half a score of homes were there
And in one a maiden fair
Held the heart of Billy Vanero
Vanero's Little Bess

So no wonder he grew pale
When he heard the settler's tale
Of the men that he'd seen murdered
Yesterday at Rocky Run
Sure as there's a God above
I will save the gal I love
By my love for little Bessie
I will see that somethin's done

Not a moment he delayed
When his brave resolve was made
Why man his comrades told him
When they heard of his daring plan
You are riding straight to death
But he answered save your breath
I may never reach the cow ranch
But I'll do the best I can

As he crossed the alkali
All his thoughts flew on ahead
To the little band at cow ranch
Thinking not a danger near
With his quirt's unceasing whirl
And the jingle of his spurs
Little Chapo bore the cowboy
O'er the far away frontier

Lower and lower sank the sun
He drew rein at Rocky Run
Here the men met death my Chapo
And he stroked his glossy mane
So we'll loathly go to warn
E're the coming of the morn
If we fail God help my Bessie
And he started on again

Sharp and clear a rifle shot
Woke the echoes of the spot
I am wounded cried Vanero
As he swayed from side to side
While there's life there's always hope
Slowly onward I will lope
If I fail to reach the cow ranch
Bessie Lee shall know I tried

I will save her yet he cried
Bessie Lee shall know I tried
And for her sake then he halted
In the shadow of a hill
From his buckskin shirt he took
With weak hands a little book
For a blank leaf from its pages
Saying this shall be my will

From a limb a pen he broke
And he dipped his pen of oak
In the warm blood that was spurting
From a wound above his heart
Rouse he wrote before too late
Apache warriors lie in wait
Goodbye God bless you darling
And he felt the cold tears start

Then he made his message fast
Love's first message and its last
To the saddle horn he tied it
And his lips were white with pain
Take this message if not me
Straight to little Bessie Lee
Then he leaned down in the saddle
And touched the sweaty mane

Just at dusk a horse of brown
Wet with sweat came panting down
The little lane at the cow ranch
Stopped in front of Bessie's door
But the cowboy was asleep
And his slumber was so deep
Little Bess could never wake him
Though she tried forever more

You have heard this story told
By the young and by the old
Down yonder at the cow ranch
The night the Apaches came
Of the sharp and bloody fight
How the chief fell in the flight
Of the panic-stricken warriors
When they heard Vanero's name

Gillette Brothers *"Cinch Up Your Riggin'"* 1994

Cowboy Songs Old & New

Bil-ly Va - ne - ro heard them say in an Ar - i - zo-na town one day,   that a

band of A-pa-che Ind-ians were   on the trail of   death.   Heard them

tell of mur - der done,   three men   killed at   Ro - cky   Run.   They're in

dan - ger at the cow ranch said Va - ne - ro un-der his   breath.

BRAVEST COWBOY

I am the bravest cowboy that ever trod the West
I've been all 'round the Rockies, got bullets in my breast

In eighteen hundred and sixty-three I joined the immigrant band
We marched from San Antonio down by the Rio Grande

I went out on the prairie, I learned to rope and line
I learned to pocket money, but I did not dress much fine

I rambled down to Texas, where I learned to rob and steal
And when I robbed that cowboy, how happy I did feel

I wore a wide brim high hat, my saddle too was fine
And when I courted that pretty young girl you know I called her mine

I courted her for beauty, for love it was in vain
They carried me down to Dallas to wear a ball and chain

Paul Friedman and Jody Kruskal *"Paul & Jody"* 2010

Cowboy Songs Old & New

I am the bra-vest cow-boy that ev - er trod the West. I've

been all a-round the Rock-ies, got bul-lets in my breast.

THE BRAZOS RIVER SONG

We crossed the wide Pecos
Forded the Nueces
We swam the Guadalupe
And floated down the Brazos
Red River runs rusty
The Wichita clear
But it's down by the Brazos
I courted my dear

LI, LI, LI, LEE, LEE, LEE
GIVE ME YOUR HAND
LI, LI, LI, LEE, LEE, LEE
GIVE ME YOUR HAND
LI, LI, LI, LEE, LEE, LEE
GIVE ME YOUR HAND
MANY A RIVER
THAT WATERS THE LAND

We see Angelina
Goes gleaming and gliding
The crooked Colorado
Is weaving and winding
The slow San Antonio
Courses the plain
But I never will ride
By the Brazos again

She kissed me, she hugged me
She called me her dandy
Oh the Trinity is muddy
And the Brazos quicksandy
She kissed me, she hugged me
She called me her own
But it's down by the Brazos
She left me alone

The girls on Little River
Are plump and they're pretty
On the Sabine and the Sulphur
There's many a beauty
Along the ol' Canadian
There's girls by the score
But I never will ride
By the Brazos no more

Gillette Brothers "Many Long Miles to Ride" 2006

Cowboy Songs Old & New

Verse

We crossed the wide Pe-cos, we forded the Nu - e-ces, we swam the Gua-da-
lu - pe and floa-ted down the Bra-zos. Red Ri-ver runs rus-ty the
Wi-chi-ta clear. But it's down by the Bra-zos I cour-ted my dear.

Chorus

LI, LI, LI, LEE, LEE, LEE, GIVE ME YOUR HAND. LI, LI, LI,
LEE, LEE, LEE, GIVE ME YOUR HAND. LI, LI, LI, LEE, LEE, LEE,
GIVE ME YOUR HAND. MA-NY A RI-VER THAT WA-TERS THIS LAND.

BUCKING BRONCO

Belle Starr (c.1878)

My love is a rider, wild horses he breaks
But he's promised to quit it and just for my sake
Oh he ties up one foot and the saddle puts on
A swing and a jump and he's mounted and gone

The first time I seen him was early one spring
He was ridin' a bronco, a high-headed thing
Oh he tipped me a wink as he gaily did go
For he wished me to look at his bucking bronco

The next time I seen him was late in the fall
He was swinging the gals down at Tomlinson's Hall
We laughed and we talked as we danced to and fro
He promised never to ride on another bronco

He gave me some presents among them a ring
The return that I made was a far better thing
Was a young maiden's heart I would have you to know
He won it by riding his bucking bronco

My love has a gun and that gun he can use
But he's quit his gunfighting as well as his booze
He's sold off his saddle his gun and his rope
There's no more gunfighting and that's what I hope

Now all you young maidens where e'er you reside
Beware of the cowboy that swings the rawhide
He'll court you and pet you and off he will go
Up the trail in the spring on his bucking bronco

Gillette Brothers *"Lone Star Trail"* 1997

Cowboy Songs Old & New

My love is a ri - der, wild hor - ses he breaks. But he's

pro - mised to quit it and just for my sake. Oh he

ties up one foot and the sad - dle puts on. A

swing and a jump and he's moun - ted and gone.

BUFFALO GAL

As I was a-ridin' down the street
Down the street, down the street
A pretty gal I chanced to meet
Under the silvery moon

BUFFALO GAL WON'T YOU COME OUT TONIGHT
COME OUT TONIGHT, COME OUT TONIGHT
BUFFALO GAL WON'T YOU COME OUT TONIGHT
AND DANCE BY THE LIGHT OF THE MOON

I asked her if she'd stop and talk
Stop and talk, stop and talk
Her feet covered up the whole sidewalk
She was fair to view

I asked her if she'd be my wife
Be my wife, be my wife
Then I'd be happy all my life
If she would marry me

Gene Autry *"Cow Town"* 1950

Verse

As I was a-ri-din' down the street, down the street, down the street. A

pret-ty gal I chanced to meet un-der the sil-ve-ry moon.

Chorus

BUF-FA-LO GAL WON'T YOU COME OUT TO-NIGHT,

COME OUT TO-NIGHT, COME OUT TO-NIGHT.

BUF-FA-LO GAL WON'T YOU COME OUT TO-NIGHT AND

DANCE BY THE LIGHT OF THE MOON.

THE CHUCKWAGON'S MIRED

Come wrangle your bronco and saddle him quick
The cookie's in trouble down there by the crick
So cinch up your riggin' you bronc-stomping runts
And pull 'em so tight that your cow pony grunts

We'll need all the punchers the foreman can send
'Cause the chuckwagon's mired down there by the bend
The cattle are scattered all over the plain
While waddies are yelling in language profane

Let 'em spread out boys the cook's in a fuss
The quicksands are causing this feller to cuss
But this is the time every waddie's his friend
The chuckwagon's mired down there by the bend

Come with your ropes that are heavy and stout
No grub for the boys till the wagon's pulled out
It's in to the hubs and it's sinking down slow
While cookie is a cussin' and watching it go

Come hustle you punchers and give us a hand
Before we are conquered by water and sand
A-straining of ropes and a-gruntin' of nags
And woe to the waddie whose riata sags

It's spur 'em and quirt 'em and make 'em lay to
And now she is moving and now she is through
It's worth all the time that the effort requires
'Cause there's nothing to eat when the chuckwagon's mired

Gillette Brothers *"Cinch Up Your Riggin'"* 1994

Cowboy Songs Old & New

Come wran-gle your bron-co and sad-dle him quick. The

coo-kie's in trou-ble down there by the crick. So

cinch up your rig-gin' you bronc-stom-ping runts. And

pull 'em so tight that your cow po - ny grunts.

CIELITO LINDO

Quirino Mendoza y Cortés (1882)

De la Sierra Morena
Cielito lindo, vienen bajando
Un par de ojitos negros
Cielito lindo, de contrabando

AY, AY, AY, AY
CANTA Y NO LLORES
PORQUE CANTANDO SE ALEGRAN
CIELITO LINDO, LOS CORAZONES

Pájaro que abandona
Cielito lindo, su primer nido
Si lo encuentra ocupado
Cielito lindo, bien merecido

Ese lunar que tienes
Cielito lindo, junto a la boca
No se lo des a nadie
Cielito lindo, que a mí me toca

Una flecha en el aire
Cielito lindo, lanzó Cupido
Si la tiró jugando
Cielito lindo, a mí me ha herido

Quirino Mendoza y Cortes (1882)

Verse: De la Si - er-ra Mor - en - a ci - e - li - to lin-do vi - en-en ba - jan-do.

Un par de o - ji-tos ne - gros, cie - li - to lin-do de con - tra-ban - do.

Chorus: AY, AY, AY, AY. CAN - TA NO LLO-RES. POR-

QUE CAN-TAN-DO SE A-LE-GRAN. CIE-LI-TO LIN-DO LOS COR-A-ZO-NES.

COCINERO

Fran Hedrick / Pipp Gillette

He said my chest is hurtin' mighty bad
I got to lay me down
No need to fetch a doctor boys
'Cause it's too far to town
I can tell you now
This battle I won't win
The head patron is callin'
This old cocinero in

Oh turn my skillets upside down
Put my flour away
Put those beans back in the sack
They'll not get cooked today
I've cooked you lots of grub boys
Rolled out lots of dough
I got to roll my bed now
Time for me to go

I'LL NOT GET UP
AND COOK FOR YOU
NO MORE AT 4 AM
THE HEAD PATRON IS CALLIN'
THIS OLD COCINERO IN

[Bridge]
I HOPE THEY HAVE A CAMPFIRE
AND A GOOD CHUCKBOX UP THERE
SO I CAN SIT AROUND ALL DAY
AND COOK MY COUNTRY FARE

I've made a list of cowboys
To carry me to my rest
I wish I could have picked you all
For I have known the best
And I hope you boys build a campfire tonight
And lift a glass
And drink to those good memories
We've made in the past

GOODBYE BOYS
GOD BLESS YOU ALL
UNTIL WE MEET AGAIN
THE HEAD PATRON IS CALLIN'
THIS OLD COCINERO IN

Then he closed his eyes in death
In gentle sleep
While we all gathered 'round
Tryin' not to weep
We'll always remember that sad old day
That day back when
The head patron did call our
Old cocinero in

Gillette Brothers "Cinch Up Your Riggin'" 1994

Fran Hedrick, Pipp Gillette

Verse

He said my chest is hur-tin' migh-ty bad. I got to lay me down.

No need to fetch a doc-tor boys, 'cause it's too far to town.

I can tell you now this bat-tle I won't win.

The head pa-tron is cal-lin' this old co-ci-ne-ro in.

Refrain

I'LL NOT GET UP AN COOK FOR YOU NO MORE AT FOUR A. M.

THE HEAD PA-TRON IS CAL-LIN' THIS OLD CO-CI-NE-RO-IN.

Bridge

I HOPE THEY HAVE A CAMP-FIRE AND A GOOD CHUCK-BOX UP THERE.

SO I CAN SIT A-ROUND ALL DAY AND COOK MY COUN-TRY FARE.

© 1994 Fran Hedrick, Pipp Gillette
Used with Permission, All Rights Reserved

THE COLORADO TRAIL

Ride all the lonely nights
Ride through the day
Keep the herd a'movin' on
Movin' on its way

WEEP ALL YE LITTLE RAINS
WAIL WINDS WAIL
ALL ALONG, ALONG, ALONG
THE COLORADO TRAIL

Eyes like the morning sun
Cheeks like a rose
Laura was a pretty girl
God almighty knows

Ride through the stormy night
Dark is the sky
Wish I'd stayed in Abilene
Nice and warm and dry

Don Edwards *"Songs of the Trail"* 1992

Verse

| C | Am | F | C |

Ride all the lone - ly nights. Ride through the day.

| C | Am | D7 | G |

Keep the herd a - mo - vin' on. Mo - vin' on its way.

Chorus

| C | Am | Dm | C |

WEEP ALL YE LIT-TLE RAINS. WAIL, WINDS WAIL.

| C | Am | Em | Dm | G | F | C |

ALL A-LONG, A-LONG, A-LONG, THE CO - LO-RA-DO TRAIL.

COWBOY JACK

Jack was a lonely cowboy
With a heart so brave and true
He learned to love a maiden
With eyes of heaven's blue

They learned to love each other
They named their wedding day
'Til a quarrel came between them
And Jack he rode away

He joined a band of cowboys
He tried to forget her name
Out on the lonely prairie
She waits for him the same

YOUR SWEETHEART
WAITS FOR YOU JACK
YOUR SWEETHEART WAITS FOR YOU
OUT ON THE LONELY PRAIRIE
WHERE THE SKIES ARE ALWAYS BLUE

One night when work was finished
Just at the close of day
Someone said sing a song Jack
To drive all cares away

When Jack began his singing
His mind it wandered back
He was thinking of the maiden
Who waited for her Jack

YOUR SWEETHEART
WAITS FOR YOU JACK
YOUR SWEETHEART WAITS FOR YOU
OUT ON THE LONELY PRAIRIE
WHERE THE SKIES ARE ALWAYS BLUE

He left the camp next morning
Breathing his sweetheart's name
I'll go and ask forgiveness
For I know that I'm to blame

But when he reached the prairie
He found a new-made mound
His friends then sadly told him
They laid his loved one down

They said as she lay dying
She breathed her sweetheart's name
And she asked them with her last breath
To tell him when he came

YOUR SWEETHEART
WAITS FOR YOU JACK
YOUR SWEETHEART WAITS FOR YOU
OUT ON THE LONELY PRAIRIE
WHERE THE SKIES ARE ALWAYS BLUE

Gillette Brothers *"Home Ranch"* 1992

Verse & Chorus

G   C

Jack   was   a   lone - ly cow - boy,   with a
YOUR SWEET - HEART WAITS FOR YOU JACK.   YOUR

D   G

heart   so   brave   so   true.   He
SWEET - HEART WAITS FOR YOU.   OUT

G   C

learned to love a mai - den,   with
ON THE LONE - LY PRAI - RIE,   WHERE

D   G

eyes of hea - ven's blue.
SKIES ARE AL - WAYS BLUE.

THE COWBOY LIFE

The cowboy life is a dreary, dreary life
Some say it's free from care
Rounding up the cattle from morning till night
In the middle of the prairie so bare

Half-past four that noisy cook will roar
Hey boys it's the breaking of day
Slowly we rise with sleepy-feeling eyes
As the short summer night passed away

The cowboy life is a dreary, dreary life
From dawn till the setting sun
Then his day's work it is not done
For there's still his night guard to go on

The wolves and owls with their terrifying howls
Disturb us in our midnight dream
When we're layin' in our slickers on a cold rainy night
Way over on the Pecos stream

The cowboy life is a dreary, dreary life
All out in the midnight rain
Punchin' cattle from morning till night
Way out on the Texas plains

Spring sets in, our troubles all begin
The weather being fierce and cold
We're almost froze from the water on our clothes
And the cattle we can scarcely hold

Now the cowboy life is a mighty dreary life
All out in the sleet and snow
Winter time comes, he begins to think
Where did his summer wages go

I once loved to roam but now I stay at home
All you punchers take my advice
Sell your bridle and saddle, quit your roving and travels
Tie on to a pretty little wife

You can talk about your farms and your big city charms
You can talk about your silver and gold
But the cowboy life is a dreary, dreary life
When you're driving through the heat and the cold

The cowboy life is a dreary, dreary life
All out in the heat and cold
While the rich man is sleeping on his velvet couch
Dreaming of his silver and gold
Don Edwards "The Best of Don Edwards" 1998

The cow-boy life is a drea-ry, drea-ry life. Some say it's free from care.

Round-ing up the cat-tle from mor - ning till night, in the mid-dle of the prai-rie so bare.

COWBOY'S DREAM

Charley Hart (1873)

Last night as I lay on the prairie
And gazed at the stars in the sky
I wondered if ever a cowboy
Would drift to that sweet by and by

ROLL ON, ROLL ON
ROLL ON LITTLE DOGIES ROLL ON, ROLL ON
ROLL ON, ROLL ON
ROLL ON LITTLE DOGIES ROLL ON

They say there will be a great roundup
And the cowboys like dogies will stand
To be marched by the riders of judgement
Who are posted and know every brand

I wonder if ever a cowboy
Stood ready for that judgement day
And to say to the Boss of the Riders
I am ready come drive me away

The Sons of the Pioneers "Standard Radio Transcriptions" 1935

Verse

Last night as I lay on the prai-rie, and gazed at the stars in the sky. I

won-dered if ev-er a cow-boy, would drift to that sweet by and by.

Chorus

ROLL ON, ROLL ON, ROLL ON LIT-TLE DO-GIES ROLL ON, ROLL ON.

ROLL ON, ROLL ON, ROLL ON LIT-TLE DO-GIES ROLL ON.

THE COWMAN'S PRAYER

Lord please help me, lend me Thine ear
The prayer of a troubled cowman to hear
No doubt my prayer to you may seem strange
But I want you to bless my cattle range

Bless the roundups year by year
Please then don't forget the growing steer
Water the land with brooks and rills
For my cattle that roam on a thousand hills

Now O Lord, if you'll be so good
See that my stock has plenty of food
Our mountains are peaceful, the prairies serene
Oh Lord, for the cattle, please keep them green

Prairie fires, won't you please stop?
Make thunder roll and water to drop
It frightens me to see the dread smoke
Unless it is stopped, I'm bound to go dead broke

As you, O Lord, my fine herds behold
They represent a sack of pure gold
I think that at least five cents on the pound
Would be a good price for beef the year round

One thing more, and then I'll be through
Instead of one calf let my cows have two
I may pray different from all other men
But I've had my say, and now, amen

Roy Rogers & Dale Evans *"16 Great Songs of the Old West"* 1949

Cowboy Songs Old & New

Oh Lord please help me, lend me Thine ear. The prayer of a trou - bled cow - man to hear. No doubt my pray - er to you may seem strange, but I want you to bless my cat - tle range.

CURLEY JOE

One mile below Blue Canyon on a lonely piñon trail
Near the little town of Sanctos nestled in a quiet dale
Is the grave of a young cowboy whose name is now unknown
Save by a few frontiersmen who call the spot their own

He was as fine a rider as ever forked a steed
He was brave and kind and generous, never did a dirty deed
Curley Joe's the name he went by, 'twas enough none cared to know
If he ever had another so they called him Curley Joe

Three miles from Sanctos village lived an ex-grandee of Spain
And his daughter bonny Enza called the White Rose of the Plain
Curley loved this high-born lassie since that time so long ago
When he found her on the mountain lost and blinded by the snow

But coquettish was fair Enza, 'tis a woman's foolish trait
That has blasted many a manhood like the harsh decrees of fate
When pressed in earnest language not flowery but sincere
In an answer to his question she smiled and shed a tear

Dear Curley Joe amigo, quite wearisome you grow
Your sister, sir forever, but your wife no never, Joe
Not another word was spoken in a week poor Joe was dead
Killed by a bucking bronco or at least that's what they said

For many a year the tombstone that marked this cowboy's grave
In quaint and curious language this prophetic warning gave
Never hope to win the daughter of the boss who owns the brand
I tried it and changed ranges to a far and better land

Gillette Brothers "Cinch Up Your Riggin'" 1994

Cowboy Songs Old & New

One mile be-low Blue Can-yon on a lone-ly pin-yon trail, near the lit-tle town of Sanc-tos nes-tled in a qui-et dale. Is the grave of a young cow-boy whose name is now un-known, save by a few fron-tiers-men who call the spot their own.

THE DEVIL MADE TEXAS

Oh the devil in hell they say he was chained
And there for a thousand years he remained
He neither complained nor did he groan
But decided to start up a hell of his own

Where he could torment the souls of men
Without being shut in a prison pen
So he asked the Lord if he had any sand
Left over from making of this great land

The Lord He said yes I got plenty on hand
But it's way down south on the Rio Grande
And to tell you the truth the stuff is so poor
I doubt it will do for hell anymore

The Devil went down and looked over the truck
And he said if it came as a gift he was stuck
For after he'd examined it careful and well
He decided the place was too dry for a hell

But the Lord just to get the stuff off His hands
He promised the Devil He'd water the lands
For He had some old water that was of no use
A regular bog hole that stunk like the deuce

So the grant was made, the deed it was given
The Lord he returned to his place up in heaven
The Devil soon saw he had everything needed
To start up a hell and so he proceeded

He scattered tarantulas over the roads
Put thorns on the cactus and horns on the toads
He sprinkled the sand with millions of ants
So the man that sits down must wear soles on his pants

He lengthened the horns of the Texas steer
And added an inch to the jackrabbit's ear
He put water puppies in all of the lakes
And under the rocks he put rattlesnakes

He hung thorns and brambles on all of the trees
He mixed up the dust with chiggers and fleas
The rattlesnakes bites you, the scorpion stings
The mosquito delights you by buzzing his wings

The heat in the summer's a hundred and ten
Too cool for the devil and too hot for men
And all who remained in that climate soon bore
Stings, bites and scratches and blisters galore

He quickened the buck of the bronco steed
And poisoned the feet of the centipede
The wild boar roams in the black chaparral
It's a hell of a place that we've got for a hell

He planted red peppers beside all the brooks
The Mexicans use them in all that they cook
Just dine with a Texican and you will shout
I've got hell on the inside as well as the out

Gillette Brothers "Lone Star Trail" 1997

Oh the de - vil in hell, they say he was chained, and there for a thou - sand years he re - mained. He nei - ther com - plained, nor did he groan, but de - ci - ded to start up a hell of his own.

DIAMOND JOE

Old Diamond Joe was a rich old jay
Had lots of cowboys in his pay
He rode the range with his cowboy band
And many a maverick wore his brand

If I was as rich as Diamond Joe
I'd work today and I'd work no mo'
For they work so hard and they pay so slow
I don't give a damn if I work or no

ROLL ON BOYS ROLL
DON'T YOU ROLL SO SLOW
YOU ROLL LIKE CATTLE
NEVER ROLLED BEFORE

I left my gal in a Texas shack
Told her I was coming back
But then I lost a charge and I got in jail
Found myself on the Chisholm Trail

I'll stay with the herd till they reach the end
Draw all my time and blow it in
Just one more spree and one more jail
I'll head right back that lonesome trail

ROLL ON BOYS ROLL
DON'T YOU ROLL SO SLOW
YOU ROLL LIKE CATTLE
NEVER ROLLED BEFORE

I'll cross old Red at the Texas line
Head straight back to that gal of mine
I'll sit in the shade and sing my song
And watch the herds as they move along

When my summons come to leave this world
I'll say goodbye to my little girl
I'll fold my hands when it's time to go
And say farewell to Diamond Joe

Gillette Brothers "Home Ranch" 1992
Gillette Brothers "Many Long Miles to Ride" 2006

Verse

Old Dia - mond Joe was a rich old jay,
If I was rich as Dia - mond Joe,

had lots of cow - boys in his pay.
I'd work to - day and I'd work no more.

He rode the range with his cow - boy band,
For they work so hard and they pay so slow,

and many a mav - erick wore his brand. ROLL
I don't give a damn if work or no.

Chorus

ON BOYS ROLL, DON'T YOU ROLL SO SLOW. YOU

ROLL LIKE CAT - TLE NE - VER ROLLED BE - FORE.

DONEY GAL

We're alone Doney Gal in the rain and hail
Got to drive these dogies down the trail

IT'S RAIN OR SHINE
SLEET OR SNOW
ME AND MY DONEY GAL
ARE ON THE GO
YES, RAIN OR SHINE
SLEET OR SNOW
ME AND MY DONEY GAL
ARE BOUND TO GO

We'll ride the range from sun to sun
For a cowboy's work is never done
He's up and gone at the break of day
Drivin' the dogies on their weary way

A cowboy's life is a weary thing
For it's rope and brand and ride and sing
Yes, day or night in the rain or hail
He'll stay with his dogies out on the trail

Rain or shine, sleet or snow
Me and my Doney Gal are on the go
We travel down that lonesome trail
Where a man and his horse seldom ever fail

We whoop at the sun and yell through the hail
But we drive the poor dogies on down the trail
And we'll laugh at the storms, the sleet and snow
When we reach the little town of San Antonio

Traveling up the lonesome trail
Where a man and his horse seldom fail
Jogging along through fog and dew
Wish for sunny days and you

Over the prairies lean and brown
On through the wastes where there ain't no town
Swimming the rivers across our way
We fight on forward day-end on day

Trailing the herd through mountains green
We pen the cattle in Abilene
Round the camp-fire's flickering glow
We sing the songs of long ago

Intro

We're a-lone Do-ney Gal in the rain and hail, got to drive these do-gies down the trail. We'll

Verse

ride the range from sun to sun, for a cow-boy's work is ne-ver done. He's

up and gone at break of day, dri-vin' the do-gies on their wea-ry way. IT'S

Chorus

RAIN OR SHINE, SLEET OR SNOW, ME AND MY DO-NEY GAL ARE ON THE GO. YES

RAIN OR SHINE, SLEET OR SNOW, ME AND MY DO-NEY GAL ARE BOUND TO GO.

DOWN IN THE VALLEY

Down in the valley
The valley so low
Hang your head over
Hear the wind blow

Hear the wind blow love
Hear the wind blow
Hang your head over
Hear the wind blow

Roses love sunshine
Violets love dew
Angels in heaven
Know I love you

If you don't love me
Love whom you please
Put your arms round me
Give my heart ease

Give my heart ease love
Give my heart ease
Put your arms round me
Give my heart ease

Write me a letter
Sent it by mail
Send it in care of
The Birmingham jail

Build me a castle
Forty feet high
So I can see her
As she rides by

As she rides by love
As she rides by
So I can see her
As she rides by

Down in the valley
The valley so low
Hang your head over
Hear the wind blow

Down in the val - ley, the val - ley so low.

Hang your head o - ver, hear the wind blow.

THE DREARY BLACK HILLS

Kind friends listen here to my pitiful tale
I'm an object of pity and looking quite stale
I gave up my job selling Wright's Patent Pills
To prospect for gold in these dreary Black Hills

SO DON'T GO AWAY, STAY AT HOME IF YOU CAN
STAY AWAY FROM THAT CITY, THEY CALL IT CHEYENNE
FOR OLD SITTIN' BULL AND CHIEF WALLIPEE BILL
THEY'LL LIFT UP YOUR HAIR IN THEM DREARY BLACK HILLS

As I was out ridin' one mornin' in May
As I was out ridin' one morning for a day
I met General Custer and Buffalo Bill
They claimed they'd found gold in them dreary Black Hills

Well I got to Cheyenne but no gold did I find
Thought of the lunch route that I'd left behind
Through rain, hail, and snow, frozen plumb to the gills
They call me the orphan of the dreary Black Hills

Oh I wish that the feller that started this sell
Was a captive and Crazy Horse had him in hell
There's no use in grieving or swearing like pitch
But a man that would stay here's a son of a bitch

The roundhouse at Cheyenne is filled every night
With loafers and bummers of most every plight
On their backs is no clothes, in their pockets no bills
And each day they keep startin' for the dreary Black Hills

Jim Ringer "Waiting for the Hard Times to Go" 1972

Verse

Kind friends lis-ten here to my pi-ti-ful tale. I'm an ob-ject of pi-ty and look-ing quite stale. I

gave up my job sel-ling Wright's Pat-ent Pills to pros-pect for gold in these drea-ry Black Hills. SO

Chorus

DON'T GO A - WAY, STAY HOME IF YOU CAN. STAY A -

WAY FROM THAT CI - TY, THEY CALL IT CHEY - ENNE. FOR

OLD SIT - TIN' BULL AND CHIEF WAL - LI - PEE BILL, THEY'LL

LIFT UP YOUR HAIR IN THEM DREA-RY BLACK HILLS.

GIT ALONG LITTLE DOGIES

As I went out walking one morning for pleasure
I spied a cowboy out riding along
His hat was throwed back and his spurs were a-jinglin'
And as he approached he was singin' this song

WHOOPEE TI YI YO, GIT ALONG, LITTLE DOGIES
IT'S YOUR MISFORTUNE AND NONE OF MY OWN
WHOOPEE TI YI YO, GIT ALONG LITTLE DOGIES
KNOW THAT WYOMING WILL BE YOUR NEW HOME

Well it's early in spring when we round up them dogies
Mark 'em and brand 'em and bob off their tails
Round up the horses, load up the chuck wagon
Throw them dogies out on the long trail

Well some boys they go up the trail for pleasure
Well that's where they get it most awfully wrong
They have no idea the troubles they give us
As we go driving them dogies along

Your mother was raised way down in Texas
Where the jimson weed and the sand-burrs grow
We'll fill you up on prickly pear and cholla
Till you are ready for Idaho

Oh it's you'll be soup for Uncle Sam's Injuns
It's beef, heap beef, we hear them cry
Git along, git along, git along, little dogies
You're going to be beef steers in the sweet by and by

Gillette Brothers "Cowboys, Minstrels and Medicine Shows" 2010

Cowboy Songs Old & New

Verse

As I went out walk-ing one mor-ning for plea-sure I spied a cow-boy out ri-ding a-long. His

hat was throwed back and his spurs were a-jing-lin'and as he ap-proached he was singin' this song. WHOO-PEE

Chorus

TI YI YO, GIT A-LONG LIT-TLE DO-GIES. IT'S

YOUR MIS-FOR-TUNE AND NONE OF MY OWN. WHOO-PEE

TI YI YO, GIT A-LONG LIT-TLE DO-GIES.

KNOW THAT WY - O-MING WILL BE YOUR NEW HOME.

GOIN' TO THE WEST

In this fair land I'll stay no more
Here labor is in vain
I'll leave the mountains of my birth
And seek the fertile plains
I'm goin' to the West

YOU SAY YOU WILL NOT GO WITH ME
YOU TURN YOUR EYES AWAY
YOU SAY YOU WILL NOT FOLLOW ME
NO MATTER WHAT I SAY
BUT I'M GOIN' TO THE WEST

Three years have gone since we first met
Since I became your bride
Now I must journey far away
Without you by my side
I'm goin' to the West

I'll leave you here in this land you love
That seems so bright and fair
Where fragrant flowers are blooming
And music fills the air
I'm goin' to the West

Steve Hartz *"By the Muddy Angelina"* 2010

Verse

In this fair land   I'll stay no more.   Here la - bor is in vain.   I'll

leave the moun-tains of my birth and seek the fer-tile plains. I'm go-in' to the West.

Chorus

YOU SAY YOU WILL NOT GO WITH ME,   YOU TURN YOUR EYES A-WAY. YOU SAY YOU

WILL NOT FOL-LOW ME NO MAT-TER WHAT I SAY.   I'M GO-IN' TO THE WEST.

THE GOUGE-EYE SALOON

Steve Hartz

From the Gouge Eye Saloon on the old Neches River
There's stories they tell that would make a heart shiver
Where they're all running wild and they ain't on the level
And to walk through those doors is to dance with the devil

SO DON'T GO
DON'T YOU GO RAMBLIN'
DARLIN' DON'T YOU GO A-GAMBLIN'
THERE'S MORE FISH IN THESE HERE WATERS
IF YOU GO I MIGHT CATCH ME ANOTHER

There's a fire in the stove now your mule don't need hitchin'
Get your ole fiddl-i-o we'll dance in the kitchen
The sun's sinkin' red as a new copper penny
There's cornbread and catfish and coffee a-plenty

And when the moon's shining down through the great mossy tangles
And your old banjo rings, it sings and it jangles
I'll sing right along and you won't have to ask me
In our old shanty shack I'll make you so happy

Cowboy Songs Old & New

Steve Hartz

Verse

From the Gouge Eye Sa - loon on the old Ne - ches Ri - ver, there's
sto - ries they tell that would make a heart shiver. Where they're
all run - ning wild and they ain't on the le - vel, and to
walk through those doors is to dance with the de - vil. SO

Chorus

DON'T GO, DON'T YOU GO RAM-BLIN', DAR - LIN' DON'T YOU GO A GAM-BLIN' THERE'S
MORE FISH IN THESE HERE WA-TERS IF YOU GO I MIGHT CATCH ME A - NO-THER.

THE GREAT WESTERN WOODS

Steve Hartz

We come down from Alabama
In the spring of '43
Daddy'd heard those tales of Texas
And the Great Western Woods he would see

Folks they come from 'round the county
Wished us well with final words
Fiddles ringin' 'cross the cornfield
Stirrin' somethin' in my soul I'd never heard

YEARS HAD COME AND YEARS HAD GONE
WORKED OUR FINGERS TO THE BONE
DADDY DONE THE BEST HE COULD
AN' LEFT THAT ALABAMA FARM FOR THE WESTERN WOODS

Loaded on that gray-board wagon
Everything we ever owned
And as we bogged down in the Paint Rock
Well I swear those oxen give the loudest groan

Rocky pass and muddy mire
Weary souls put to the test
Like the dream once crossed the ocean
There's a land of milk and honey in the West

Ole horse flies and buffalo gnats
Praying' for the wind to blow
With fevered brow they come up pleading
To the Great Western Woods you must go

[Bridge]
NOW I WORK THESE OLE LOGS IN MY HOBNAILED SHOES
AND I RIDE AS A DROVER SOMETIMES
AN' MOTHER AND DAD THEY'RE ASLEEP IN THE CLAY
JUST A MILE BEYOND THE LOUISIANA LINE

Steve Hartz *"Settlers of the Western Woods"* 2012

Cowboy Songs Old & New

Steve Hartz

Verse

We come down from A-la-ba-ma, in the spring of for-ty three. Dad-dy'd
heard those tales of Te-xas, and the Great Wes-tern Woods he would see. Folks they
come from 'round the coun-try, wished us well with fi-nal words. Fid-dles
ring - in' cross the corn-field, stir-rin' some-thin' in my soul I'd ne-ver heard. YEARS HAD

Chorus

COME AND YEARS HAD GONE, WORKED OUR FIN - GERS TO THE BONE. DAD-DY
DONE THE BEST HE COULD AN' LEFT THAT A-LA-BA-MA FARM FOR THE WES-TERN WOODS.

Bridge

Work these ole logs in my hob-nail-ed shoes, and I ride as a dro-ver some times. An'
mo-ther and dad they're a-sleep in the clay, just a mile be-yond the Lou-i-si-an-a line.

GREEN GROW THE LILACS

I used to have a sweetheart but now I've got none
Since she's gone and left me I care not for one
Since she's gone and left me contented I'll be
For she loves another one better than me

GREEN GROW THE LILACS ALL SPARKLING WITH DEW
I'M LONELY MY DARLING SINCE PARTIN' WITH YOU
AND BY OUR NEXT MEETING I HOPE TO PROVE TRUE
AND CHANGE THE GREEN LILACS TO THE RED, WHITE AND BLUE

I passed my love's window both early and late
The look that she gave me it made my heart ache
The look that she gave me was painful to see
For she loves another one better than me

I wrote my love a letter in rosy red lines
She sent me an answer all twisted and twined
Saying keep your love letters and I will keep mine
Write to your sweetheart and I'll write to mine

GREEN GROW THE LI - LACS ALL SPARK - LING WITH DEW. I'M

LONE - LY MY DAR - LING SINCE PAR - TIN' WITH YOU. AND

BY OUR NEXT MEET - ING I HOPE TO PROVE TRUE, AND

CHANGE THE GREEN LI - LACS TO THE RED WHITE AND BLUE.

THE HIGH-TONED DANCE

James Barton Adams (1919)

Now you can't expect a cowboy to agitate his shanks
In an etiquettish manner in aristocratic ranks
When he's always been accustomed to shake the heel and toe
At the rattling rowdy dances where much etiquette don't go
You can bet I set them laughin' in quite an excited way
A giving of their squinters an astonished sort of play
When I happened into Denver and was asked to take a prance
In the smooth and easy measures of a high-toned dance

When I got among the ladies in their frocks of fleecy white
And the dudes togged out in wrappings that was simply out of sight
Tell you what I was embarrassed and how I couldn't keep
From feeling like a burro in a pretty flock of sheep
Every step I made was awkward, I blushed a fiery red
Like the principal adornment on a turkey gobbler's head
The ladies said 'twas seldom that they had ever had a chance
To see an old-time puncher at a high-toned dance

I cut me out a heifer from the bunch of purty girls
And I yanked her to the center to dance those dreamy whirls
She laid her head upon my shoulder in a lovin' sort of way
And we drifted into heaven as the band began to play
I could feel my neck a burning from her nose a-breathing heat
As she do-si-do'd around me, half the time upon my feet
She peered up in my blinkers with a soul-dissolving glance
Quite conducive to the pleasures of a high-toned dance

Every nerve just got to dancing to the music of delight
Oh I hugged that little sage-hen, you bet I held her tight
But she never made a beller and the glances of her eyes
Seemed to thank me for the pleasures of a genuine surprise
She cuddled up against me in a loving sort of way
And I hugged her all the tighter for her trustifying play
Tell you what, the joys of heaven ain't a cussed circumstance
To the huggamania pleasures of a high-toned dance

When they struck the old cotillion on the music bill of fare
Every bit of devil in me seemed to burst out on a tear
Well I fetched a cowboy whoopee and I started in to rag
And I cut her with my trotters 'til the floor began to sag
My partner she got sea sick and rushed to grab a seat
I balanced for the next one but she dodged me slick and neat
Tell you what, I took the creases from my go-to-meeting pants
When I put the cowboy trimmin's on that high-toned dance

Gillette Brothers *"Cinch Up Your Riggin'"* 1994

Cowboy Songs Old & New

First Verse

Now you can't ex-pect a cow-boy to ag-i-tate his shanks in an e-ti-quet-tish man-ner in a-ris-to-cra-tic ranks. When he's al-ways been ac-cust-omed to shake the heel and toe at the rat-tling row-dy dan-ces where much e-ti-quette don't go. You can

All Others

bet I set them laugh-in' in quite an ex-ci-ted way, a giv-ing of their squin-ters an a-ston-ished sort of play. When I hap-pened in-to Den-ver and was asked to take a prance in the smooth and ea-sy mea-sures of a high-toned dance.

James Barton Adams

HOME ON THE RANGE

Brewster Higley / Daniel Kelley (1872), John Lomax (1910)

Oh give me a home where the buffalo roam
And the deer and the antelope play
Where seldom is heard a discouraging word
And the skies are not cloudy all day

HOME, HOME ON THE RANGE
WHERE THE DEER AND THE ANTELOPE PLAY
WHERE SELDOM IS HEARD A DISCOURAGING WORD
AND THE SKIES ARE NOT CLOUDY ALL DAY

Where the air is so pure, the zephyrs so free
The breezes so balmy and light
That I would not exchange my home on the range
For all of the cities so bright

The red man was pressed from this part of the West
He's likely no more to return
To the banks of Red River where seldom if ever
Their flickering campfires burn

How often at night when the heavens are bright
With the light from the glittering stars
Have I stood here amazed and asked as I gazed
If their glory exceeds that of ours

I love these wild prairies where I roam
The curlew I love to hear scream
And I love the white rocks and the antelope flocks
That graze on the mountaintops green

Oh give me a land where the bright diamond sand
Flows leisurely down the stream
Where the graceful white swan goes gliding along
Like a maid in a heavenly dream

Brewster Higley / Daniel Kelley (1872)

Verse

Oh give me a home where the buf-fa-lo roam, where the deer and the an-te-lope play. Where

sel-dom is heard a dis-cour-a-ging word, and the skies are not clou-dy all day.

Chorus

HOME, HOME ON THE RANGE. WHERE THE DEER AND THE AN-TE-LOPE PLAY. WHERE

SEL-DOM IS HEARD A DIS-COUR-A-GING WORD, AND THE SKIES ARE NOT CLOU-DY ALL DAY.

I RIDE AN OLD PAINT

I ride an Old Paint, I lead an Old Dan
I'm goin' to Montana for to throw the hoolihan
They feed in the coulees, they water in the draw
Their tails are all matted, their backs are all raw

RIDE AROUND LITTLE DOGIES
RIDE AROUND THEM SLOW
FOR THE FIERY AND SNUFFY
ARE RARIN' TO GO

Oh when I die take my saddle from the wall
Just put it on my pony and lead him from his stall
Tie my bones to his back, turn our faces to the West
And we'll ride the prairie that we love the best

RIDE AROUND LITTLE DOGIES
RIDE AROUND THEM SLOW
FOR THE FIERY AND SNUFFY
ARE RARIN' TO GO

Roy Rogers & Dale Evans, "*16 Great Songs of the Old West*", 1949

Cowboy Songs Old & New

Verse

I ride an Old Paint, I lead an Old Dan. I'm

goin' to Mon - ta - na to throw the hou - li - han. They

feed in the cou - lees, they wa - ter in the draw. Their

tails are all mat - ted, their backs are all raw. RIDE A -

Chorus

ROUND LIT-TLE DO - GIES RIDE A - ROUND THEM SLOW, FOR THE

FIE - RY AND SNUF-FY ARE RAR - IN' TO GO.

I'M HAPPY

Waddie Mitchell / Pipp Gillette

The day's circles rode and tallied
An' old sol is layin' low
Time mellows in that satisfyin' way
Now the evening's finally rallied
I can ponder long and slow
And I smile as we're windin' up the day

OH I'M LUCKY AND I'M HAPPY
THANKFUL I'M SO BLESSED
THE EYES I GET TO LOOK THROUGH
GAZE ON RANGES OF THE WEST
AS WE RIDE THIS GREAT ADVENTURE
WITH ITS JOYS AND ITS TRAVAILS
WITH MY COWBOY WIFE BESIDE ME
I BID ALL MY WOES FAREWELL

The old cows finance the groceries
And the ranch provides the peace
A sense of humor keeps the haunts at bay
And her love still flows artesian
All these years it's never ceased
And I know I've more than I've a right to pray

OH I'M LUCKY AND I'M HAPPY
THANKFUL I'M SO BLESSED
WE GET TO LIVE OUR LIVES
OUT ON THE RANGES OF THE WEST
WE ARE NOURISHED BY THEIR GRANDEUR
QUENCH OUR SOULS AT PRISTINE WELLS
WITH MY COWBOY WIFE BESIDE ME
WE EXPLORE THOSE HIDDEN TRAILS

We've more miles left behind us
Than we've miles left to ride
So memories mean more each passing day
And the truth that we've discovered
As we travel side by side
Is to savor all you love along the way

OH I'M LUCKY AND I'M HAPPY
THANKFUL I'M SO BLESSED
I FOUND MY PERFECT MATE
OUT ON RANGES OF THE WEST
AS WE RIDE THIS LIFE TOGETHER
OVER TIME AND THROUGH THAT VEIL
WITH MY COWBOY WIFE BESIDE ME
WE'LL RIDE THAT HEAVEN TRAIL

Cowboy Songs Old & New

Waddie Mitchell/Pipp Gillette

Verse

The day's cir-cles rode and tal-lied, an' old sol is lay-in' low. Time

mel-lows in that sa-tis-fy-in' way. Now the

eve-ning's fin-ally ral-lied, I can pon-der long and slow. And I

smile as we're wind-in' up the day. OH I'M

Chorus

LUCK-Y AND I'M HAP-PY, THANK-FUL I'M SO BLESSED, THE

EYES I GET TO LOOK THROUGH GAZE ON RAN-GES OF THE WEST. AS WE

RIDE THIS GREAT AD-VEN-TURE, WITH ITS JOYS AND ITS TRA-VAILS, WITH MY

COW-BOY WIFE BE-SIDE ME, I BID ALL MY WOES FARE-WELL.

IT COULD HAVE BEEN WORSE

Waddie Mitchell / Pipp Gillette

When the chore boy's two dogs run them steers in the bogs
Them curs an' that chore boy got cursed
Cost two days of hard work in the mud an' the murk
It weren't much fun but it could have been worse

When the ground all around you was froze slick and hard
An' your mount was all humped up an' terse
Boy you knew you'd get tried once atop that old cold hide
It weren't much fun but could have been worse

OH IT COULD HAVE BEEN WORSE
BUT IT COULD HAVE BEEN BETTER
THANK GOODNESS NOBODY GOT CRIPPLED OR KILLED
FOR YOU WEATHERED THAT STORM ALL EXCEPT THAT BROKEN ARM
AND YOU'LL BE BACK AS SOON AS YOU'RE HEALED

When that hole tipped your steed whilst you's flyin' at full speed
Hit so hard that your latigo burst
And you near broke your neck in that formidable wreck
It weren't much fun but could have been worse

And when crossin' that river that cold winter day
And the ice broke and you got immersed
Then chilled to the bone made that long trot back home
It weren't much fun but could have been worse

Now no one has a charm against them sharp rocks that arm
That rough country against all traverse
An' that bruised pastern bone made you both limp back home
It weren't much fun but could have been worse

Maybe cowboy life ain't the very best life
In the confines of this universe
But to your way of thinkin' it comes mighty close
Not quite perfect but sure could be worse

OH IT SURE COULD BE WORSE
BUT IT COULDN'T GET MUCH BETTER
ALL FUN AS LONG AS NO ONE GETS CRIPPLED OR KILLED
FOR YOU'VE SEEN MOTHER NATURE'S FULL SPLENDOR REVEALED
YOU'LL BE BACK AS SOON AS YOU'RE HEALED

Pipp Gillette "Singing Songs with Waddie & Pipp" 2015

Waddie Mitchell, Pipp Gillette

Verse

When the chore boy's two dogs run them steers in the bogs, them
ground all a - round you was froze slick and hard, your

curs and that chore boy got cursed. Cost two
mount was all humped up an terse. Boy you

days of hard work in the mud and the murk, it weren't much
knew you'd get tried once a - top that cold hide, it weren't much

fun but it could have been worse. When the
fun but it could have been worse.

OH IT

Chorus

COULD HAVE BEEN WORSE, BUT IT COULD HAVE BEEN BET-TER. THANK

GOOD-NESS NO - BO - DY GOT CRIP - PLED OR KILLED.

FOR YOU WEA-THERED THAT STORM ALL EX - CEPT THAT BRO - KEN

ARM AND YOU'LL BE BACK AS SOON AS YOU'RE HEALED.

JACK O' DIAMONDS

Jack of Diamonds, Jack of Diamonds, I know you of old
You have robbed my poor pockets of silver and gold
'Tis raining, 'tis hailing, 'tis a dark stormy night
And my horses cannot travel for the moon gives no light
My horses cannot travel for the moon gives no light

Go put up your horses and feed them some hay
Then sit down beside me till the light of the day
My horses ain't hungry, they won't eat your hay
So fair thee well, Darlin', I'll be on my way
So fair thee well, Darlin', I'll be on my way

I'll build me a cabin on the mountain so high
Where the wild geese can see me as they pass me by
As sure as the dewdrop grows on the green corn
Last night you were with me but today you are gone
Last night you were with me but today you are gone

Jack of Diamonds, Jack of Diamonds, I know you of old
You have robbed my poor pockets of silver and gold
Rye whiskey, rye whiskey, I wish you no harm
But I wish I had a bottle as long as my arm
I wish I had a bottle as long as my arm

Connie Dover "Somebody" 1991

Jack of Dia-monds, Jack of Dia-monds, I know you of old. You have

robbed my poor poc - kets of sil - ver and gold. 'Tis

rain - ing, 'tis hail - ing, 'tis a dark stor - my night. And my

hor - ses can-not tra - vel for the moon gives no light. My

hor - ses can - not tra - vel for the moon gives no light.

LEAVING CHEYENNE

Farewell fair ladies I'm leavin' Cheyenne
Farewell fair ladies I'm leavin' Cheyenne
Goodbye my little doney, my pony won't stand

OLD PAINT, OLD PAINT
I'M LEAVIN' CHEYENNE
GOODBYE OLD PAINT
I'M LEAVIN' CHEYENNE
OLD PAINT'S A GOOD PONY
AND SHE PACES WHEN SHE CAN

Last time I saw her late in the fall
She was ridin' Old Paint and leadin' Old Ball

Old Paint had a colt down on the Rio Grande
But the colt couldn't pace so they called it Cheyenne

We spread out our blankets on the green grassy ground
While the horses and the cattle were grazin' around

In the middle of the ocean there grows a green tree
I'll never prove false to the gal that loves me

With my foot in the stirrup and the bridle in my hand
Goodbye my little doney my pony won't stand

Gillette Brothers "Leaving Cheyenne" 2012

Verse

G | C

Fare - well fair la - dies I'm lea - vin' Chey - enne. Fare -

G | C | Am

well fair la - dies I'm lea - vin' Chey - enne. Good -

C | G7 | C

bye my lit - tle do - ney, my po - ny won't stand. OLD

Chorus

C | F | Am | F | G7 | C

PAINT, OLD PAINT, I'M LEA - VIN' CHEY - ENNE. GOOD -

C | F | Am | G7 | C

BYE OLD PAINT, I'M LEA - VIN' CHEY - ENNE. OLD

C | G | C | C | G | C

PAINT'S A GOOD PO - NY AND SHE PA - CES WHEN SHE CAN.

THE LILY OF THE WEST

When first I came to Louisville
My fortune for to find
I met a fair young maiden there
Her beauty filled my mind
Her rosy cheeks, her ruby lips
They gave my heart no rest
The name she bore was Flora
The Lily of the West

I courted lovely Flora
She promised ne'er to go
But soon a tale was told to me
That filled my heart with woe
They said she meets another man
Who holds my love in jest
And yet I trusted Flora
The Lily of the West

Way down in yonder shady grove
A man of low degree
He spoke unto my Flora there
And kissed her 'neath a tree
The answers that she gave to him
Like arrows pierced my breast
I was betrayed by Flora
The Lily of the West

I stepped up to my rival
My dagger in my hand
I seized him by the collar and
I ordered him to stand
All in my desperation
I stabbed him in his breast
I killed a man for Flora
The Lily of the West

I had to stand my trial
I had to make my plea
They placed me in a prisoner's dock
And then commenced on me
Although she swore my life away
Deprived me of my rest
Still I love my faithless Flora
The Lily of the West

When first I came to Lou-is-ville, my for-tune for to find. I

met a fair young mai-den there, her beau-ty filled my mind. Her

ro - sy checks, her ru-by lips, they gave my heart no rest. The

name she bore was Flo - ra, the Li-ly of the West.

THE LITTLE BLACK BULL

Little black bull come down the mountain
HOORAH JOHNNY, HOORAH JOHNNY
The little black bull come down the mountain
A LONG TIME AGO

A LONG TIME AGO
A LONG TIME AGO
THAT LITTLE BLACK BULL COME DOWN THE MOUNTAIN
A LONG TIME AGO

Well first he pawed and then he bellowed

Well he whet his horn on a white oak sapling

Well he shook his tail, he jarred the river

Well he pawed the dirt in the heifer's faces

Gillette Brothers *"Home Ranch"* 1992

Verse

Lit-tle black bull come down the moun-tain. HOO-RAH JOHN-NY, HOO-RAH JOHN-NY.

Lit-tle black bull come down the moun-tain. A LONG TIME A-GO. A

Chorus

LONG TIME A-GO, A LONG TIME A-GO. THAT

LIT-TLE BLACK BULL COME DOWN THE MOUN-TAIN, A LONG TIME A-GO.

LITTLE JOE THE WRANGLER

Jack Thorp (1898)

He was Little Joe the wrangler
He'll wrangle never more
His days with the remuda they are o'er
Was a year ago last April
He rode into our camp
Just a little Texas stray and all alone

His saddle was a Texas kack
Made many years ago
With an O.K. spur on one foot lightly slung
His bedroll in a cotton sack
Was loosely tied behind
And his canteen o'er his saddle horn was hung

He said if we would give him work
He'd do the best he could
Though he didn't know straight up about a cow
Oh the boss he cut him out a mount
And kindly put him on
'Cause he kinda liked this little kid somehow

He learned to wrangle horses
And know them all by name
Get them in by daybreak if he could
Oh to follow the chuckwagon
And always hitch the team
And help the cocinero rustle wood

We'd driven down to Pecos
The weather it being fine
We camped on the south side on a bend
When a norther started blowing
And we called out every man
For it'd taken all us hands to hold 'em in

Well Little Joe the wrangler
Was called out with the rest
Although the kid had scarcely reached the herd
When the cattle they stampeded
Like a hail storm long they fled
And we was all a-riding for the lead

Well 'neath the streaks of lightning
A rider we could see
It was Little Joe the wrangler in the lead
He was riding old Blue Rocket
With his slicker o'er his head
Trying to check the cattle in their speed

Well at last we got them milling
And kind of quieted down
And the extra guard back to the wagon went
Oh but there was one a-missin'
We knew it at a glance
Was our little Texas stray
Poor wrangling Joe

Next morning just at daybreak
We found where Rocket fell
In a washout twenty feet below
And beneath his horse mashed to a pulp
His spur had rung the knell
Was our little Texas stray
Poor wrangling Joe

Pipp Gillette, live performance at Elko Gathering, 2018

Cowboy Songs Old & New

He was Lit-tle Joe the wrang-ler, he'll wran-gle ne-ver more. His
days with the re-mu-da they are o'er. Was a
year a-go last A-pril, he rode in-to our camp. Just a
lit-tle Tex-as stray and all a-lone. His
He
sad-dle was a Tex-as kack made ma-ny years a-go, with an
said if we would give him work he'd do the best he could, though he
O. K. spur on one foot light-ly slung. His
did-n't know straight up a-bout a cow. Oh the
bed-roll in a cot-ton sack was loose-ly tied be-hind, and his
boss he cut him out a mount and kind-ly put him on, 'cause he
can-teen o'er his sad-dle horn was hung.
kind-a liked this lit-tle kid some-how.

THE LITTLE OLD SOD SHANTY

Oliver Edwin Murray (c.1880)

I'm looking rather seedy now
While holding down my claim
And my vittles are not always of the best
And the mice play shyly 'round me
As I nestle down to rest
In my little old sod shanty in the West

Oh I rather like the novelty
Of living in this way
Though my bill of fare is always rather tame
But I'm happy as a clam
On the land of Uncle Sam
In my little old sod shanty on my claim

OH THE HINGES ARE OF LEATHER
AND THE WINDOWS HAVE NO GLASS
THE BOARD ROOF LETS
THE HOWLING BLIZZARD IN
AND I HEAR THE HUNGRY KI-YOTE
AS HE SLINKS UP IN THE GRASS
'ROUND MY LITTLE OLD
SOD SHANTY ON MY CLAIM

Oh when I left my eastern home
A bachelor so gay
To try to win my way to wealth and fame
Oh I little thought that I'd come down
To burning twisted hay
In my little old sod shanty on my claim

My clothes are plastered o'er with dough
I'm looking like a fright
And everything is scattered 'round the room
But I wouldn't trade the freedom
That I have out in the West
For the table of the Eastern man's old home

Still I wish that some kind-hearted girl
Would pity on me take
And relieve me from the mess that I am in
Oh the angel how I'd bless her
If this her home she'd make
In our little old sod shanty on my claim

And we would make our fortune
On the prairies of the West
Just as happy as two lovers we'd remain
We'd forget the trials and troubles
We endured at the first
In our little old sod shanty on our claim

And if kindly fate should bless us
With now and then an heir
To cheer our hearts with honest pride of fame
Oh then we'd be contented
For the toil that we had spent
In our little old sod shanty on our claim

And as time enough had lapsed
And all those little brats
To noble man- and woman-hood had grown
Oh we wouldn't feel so lonely
As around us we would look
At our little old sod shanty on our claim

Gillette Brothers "Many Long Miles to Ride" 2006

Cowboy Songs Old & New

Oliver Edwin Murray

Verse

I'm look-ing ra-ther seed-y now while hold-ing down my claim. And my
ra-ther like the no-vel-ty of liv-ing in this way, though my

vit-tles are not al-ways of the best. And the
bill of fare is al-ways ra-ther tame. But I'm

mice play shy-ly 'round me as I nest-le down to rest, in my
hap-py as a clam on the land of Un-cle Sam, in my

lit-tle old sod shan-ty in the West. OH THE
lit-tle old sod shan-ty on my claim.

Chorus

HIN-GES ARE OF LEA-THER AND THE WIN-DOWS HAVE NO GLASS. THE

BOARD ROOF LETS THE HOWL-ING BLIZ-ZARD IN. AND I

HEAR THE HUN-GRY KI-YOTE AS HE SLINKS UP IN THE GRASS, 'ROUND MY

LIT-TLE OLD SOD SHAN-TY ON MY CLAIM.

THE LONE STAR TRAIL

I'm bound to follow the longhorn cows until I get too old
It's well I work for wages boys I get my pay in gold
My bosses they all like me they say I'm hard to beat
I spend my time in the saddle boys I'm seldom on my feet

KI-YI-YIPPEE YIPPEE-AY
KI-YI-YIPPEE YIPPEE-AY

Now I'm a Texas cowboy just off the stormy plains
My trade is girtin' saddles and pullin' bridle reins
Oh I can tip the lasso it is with graceful ease
I can rope a streak of lightnin' and ride 'er where I please

Now if I had me a little stake I soon would married be
But another week and I must go the boss said so today
My gal must gain the courage and find another one
For I'm bound to follow the Lone Star Trail until my race is run

It's when we're on the trail where the dust and bellows fly
We're fifty miles from water and the grass is scorchin' dry
The boss gets mad and ringy as you can plainly see
And I wanna leave the trail my boys and an honest farmer be

Now when we get them bedded boys we think it's for the night
Some horse will shake his saddle and give the herd a fright
They'll rise up to their feet boys and madly dash away
Then it's movin' time to the lead now boys you'll hear some cowboy say

It's when we get them rounded up and quieted down again
A dark cloud will rise in the west and fire'll play on their horns
The boss will say stay with 'em boys your pay will be in gold
I'm bound to follow the longhorn steer until I get too old

Now when I get up to Kansas I had a pleasant dream
I dreamed I was down on the Trinity down by that pleasant stream
With my true love right beside me she comes and go my bail
But I woke up broken hearted with a yearling by the tail

Now I'm a Texas cowboy just off the stormy plains
My trade is girtin' saddles and pullin' bridle reins
Oh I can tip the lasso it is with graceful ease
I can rope a streak of lightnin' and ride 'er where I please

Gillette Brothers *"Lone Star Trail"* 1997

Verse: I'm bound to follow the long-horn cows un-til I get too old. It's

well I work for wa-ges boys I get my pay in gold. My

bos-ses they all like me, they say I'm hard to beat. I

spend my time in the sad-dle boys I'm sel-dom on my feet.

Chorus: KI - YI-YIP-PEE YIP-PEE-AY. KI - YI-YIP-PEE YIP-PEE-AY.

LONG SUMMER DAY

Additional lyrics by Pipp & Guy Gillette

Long summer day make a man earn his way
LONG SUMMER DAY
Long summer day make a man earn his pay
LONG SUMMER DAY

Cornbread and bacon early in the mornin'
'FORE THE BREAK OF DAY
Hot coffee's black, rollin' and a-boilin'
'FORE THE BREAK OF DAY

Call up them horses feed 'em some corn
'FORE THE BREAK OF DAY
Saddle them horses and whistle up the dogs
'FORE THE BREAK OF DAY

Have some cornbread and bacon and tie it to your saddle
FOR THE LONG SUMMER DAY
Syrup bucket and some coffee and you tie it to your saddle
FOR THE LONG SUMMER DAY

We're lookin' for cattle in the brush and the thicket
AT THE BREAK IN THE DAY
We're lookin' for cattle in the brush and the thicket
MAKE YOU SURE EARN YOUR PAY

We're looking for screwworm, treat 'em where you find 'em
LONG SUMMER DAY
Rope 'em and tie and treat 'em where you find 'em
LONG SUMMER DAY

Dogs baying cattle in the river bottom
LONG SUMMER DAY
Dogs baying cattle and it sounds like they got 'em
NOT FAR AWAY

I'll go back home and see my Mary
AT THE END OF THE DAY
Gonna go back home and see my Mary
AT THE END OF THE DAY

Long summer day make a man earn his way
LONG SUMMER DAY
Long summer day make a man earn his pay
LONG SUMMER DAY

Gillette Brothers "Live from the Camp Street Café and Store" 2001

Long sum-mer day make a man earn his way.   LONG SUM-MER DAY.

Long sum-mer day make a man earn his pay.   LONG SUM-MER DAY.

MIDDLE OF NOWHERE

Waddie Mitchell / Pipp Gillette

Out here in the middle of nowhere
Where I'm best suited to be
Where I git rid of that somethin'
Not letting my heart and mind free
For everyone there is a somewhere
Nowhere just sits well with me
And they'd have to come out here to nowhere
If they reason to wanna see me

Never much liked the big city
They all leave me gasping for air
Feel all restricted and stranglin'
I wasn't designed to live there
Their smells and their noise can offend me
Their traffic and pace of life too
They're crammed like a tin can of sardines
Their buildings obstruct any view

But out here in the middle of nowhere
Where I've chosen to be
Nowhere suits me anywhere elsewhere
Nowhere is where I feel most free
If everyone has their own somewhere
That somewhere is nowhere for me
Unless they come out here to nowhere
They will likely not be seeing me

Their folks live on top of each other
Their water tastes strongly of bleach
Breathe air they must chew up to swallow
Reach for what's out of their reach
They'll never experience solace
Or taste of clean water and air
Unless they get out of the city
And get themselves out to nowhere

Did you ever imagine that nowhere
Might be the place you're meant to be
That nowhere just might be that somewhere
Where you can set heart and mind free
For everyone there is somewhere
Nowhere's a great place to be
And they'd have to come out here to nowhere
If they're trying to see you or me

And they'd have to come out here to nowhere
If they're trying to find you or me

Pipp Gillette "Singing Songs with Waddie & Pipp" 2015

Waddie Mitchell / Pipp Gillette

Out here in the mid-dle of no-where, where I'm best suit-ed to be.

Where I git rid of that some-thin', not let-ting my heart and mind free. For

ev-ery-one there is a some-where, no-where just sits well with me. And they'd

have to come out here to no-where if they rea-son to wan-na see me.

MUSTANG GRAY

There was a noble ranger
His name was Mustang Gray
He left his home when but a youth
Went ranging far away

BUT HE'LL GO NO MORE A-RANGING
THE SAVAGE TO AFFRIGHT
HE HAS HEARD HIS LAST WAR WHOOP
AND FOUGHT HIS LAST FIGHT

He ne'er would sleep within a tent
No comfort would he know
But like a brave old Tex-i-an
A-ranging he would go

When Texas was invaded
By a mighty tyrant foe
He mounted on his war horse
And a-ranging he did go

Once he was taken prisoner
Bound in chains along the way
He wore the yoke of bondage
Through the streets of Monterey

A senorita loved him
And followed by his side
She set him free and gave to him
Her father's steed to ride

God bless the senorita
The belle of Monterey
She opened wide the prison doors
And let him ride away

And when this veteran's life was spent
It was his last command
To bury him on Texas soil
On the banks of the Rio Grande

And there the lonely traveler
When passing by his grave
Can shed a fond and farewell tear
For the bravest of the brave

Verse

There was a no-ble ran-ger, his name was Mus-tang Gray. He

left his home when but a youth, went rang-ing far a-way. BUT HE'LL

Chorus

GO NO MORE A-RANG-ING, THE SA-VAGE TO AF-FRIGHT. HE HAS

HEARD HIS LAST WAR WHOOP AND FOUGHT HIS LAST FIGHT.

THE NIGHT-HERDING SONG

Harry Stephens (1909)

Slow up little dogies why you're roving around
You've wandered and trampled all over the ground
Oh graze along dogies and go kinda slow
And don't always be on the go
Move slow, little dogies, move slow

I have circle-herded, trail-herded, night-herded too
But to keep you together that's what I can't do
My horse is leg-weary and I'm awful tired
But if I let you get away I'm sure to get fired
Bunch up, little dogies, bunch up

Oh say little dogies when you goin' to lay down
And quit this forever shiftin' around
My limbs are weary, my seat is sore
Oh lay down, dogies like you've laid before
Lay down, little dogies, lay down

Lay still little dogies since you have laid down
Stretch away out on the big open ground
Snore loud little dogies don't mind the wild sound
It'll go when the day rolls around
Lay still, little dogies, lay still

Roy Rogers & Dale Evans *"16 Great Songs of the Old West"* 1949

Cowboy Songs Old & New

Harry Stephens

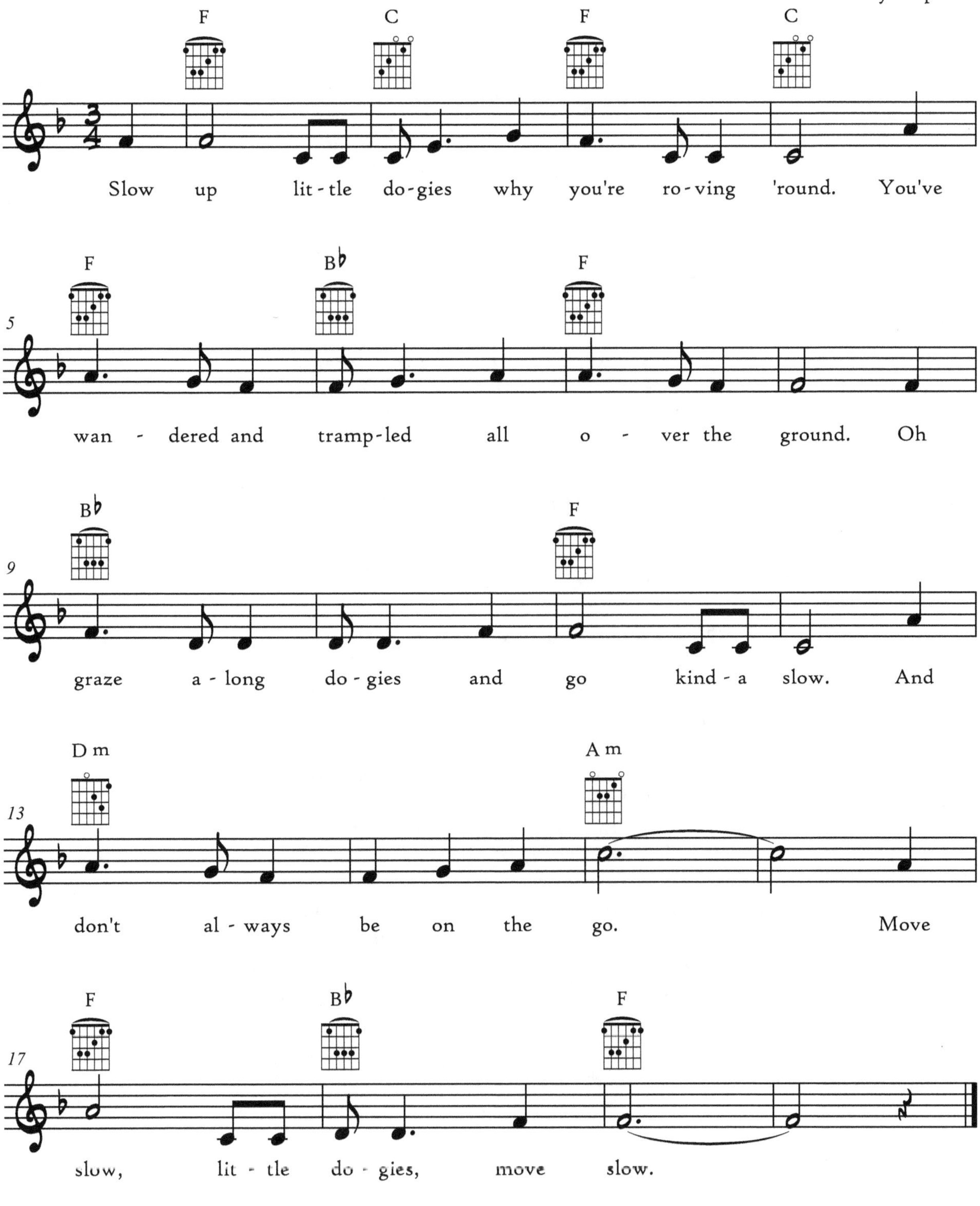

NORTH TO KANSAS

Guy & Pipp Gillette (1992)

Oh it was a fine and a pleasant day
We left Texas and the sun was glarin'
As a young cowboy with a string of horses
Off to drive the longhorns north to Kansas

Oh the work was hard and the hours were long
And the weather oh it took some bearing
Ah but we were young and we had our fun
As we drove the longhorns north to Kansas

Well we crossed the Red and the Arkansas
And the cookie he was always swearin'
And I used to sleep sittin' in my saddle
And I dreamed about the herd and Kansas

Though the drivin' rain and the blowin' wind
Just to earn your daily bread you're darin'
Left my Texas home crossed those swollen rivers
For to drive the longhorns north to Kansas

Now you're ridin' drag and you're eatin' dust
But you do your job without complainin'
Take your turn on watch like the other fellows
As we drove the longhorns north to Kansas

We arrived in Kansas in the month of June
And for Abilene we set our bearin'
With two thousand head of those rangy cattle
That we'd driven all the way to Kansas

Well I earned my keep and I paid my way
And I earned the spurs that I was wearin'
Drove a thousand miles took all kinds of chances
As we drove the longhorns north to Kansas

Gillette Brothers "Home Ranch" 1992

Oh it was a fine and a plea-sant day, we left Tex-as and the sun was glar - in'. As a young cow - boy with a string of hor - ses, off to drive the long - horns north to Kan - sas.

OCEAN OF GRASS

Guy Gillette (2012)

One stormy night while out on the trail
We were not very far from the town
When our trail boss said the cattle may stampede
And he called every hand to gather 'round

Then up spoke our trail boss of our gallant crew
And a well-spoken fellow was he
I have married me a wife in old San Antonio town
And tonight she a widow may be

OH THE OCEAN OF GRASS MAY ROLL
AND THE STORMY WINDS THEY BLOW
WHILE WE WILD COWBOYS GO RIDING FOR THE LEAD
AND THE DANCE HALL GALS BEGIN THE SHOW
AND THE DANCE HALL GALS BEGIN THE SHOW

Then up spoke the straw boss of our gallant band
And a fine looking fellow 'twas true
I care no more for my wife and my child
Than I do for the friends on this crew

Then up spoke the cook of our gallant band
And a rough looking fellow 'twas true
I will get down to work with my ovens and my stew
And we'll have plenty of grub when we're through

Well 'round and 'round went our desperate herd
And hell bent for leather went they
Oh 'round and 'round went our desperate herd
But we kept them a-millin' 'til day
Yes we kept them a-millin' 'til day

Based on the traditional song "The Mermaid" with cowboy lyrics by Guy Gillette

Gillette Brothers "Leaving Cheyenne" 2012

Guy Gillette

Verse

One stor - my night while out on the trail, we were not ve-ry far from the town. When our

trail boss said the cat-tle may stam-pede, and he called ev-ery hand to gath-er 'round. OH THE

Chorus

O - CEAN OF GRASS MAY ROLL, AND THE STOR - MY WINDS THEY

BLOW. WHILE WE WILD COW-BOYS GO RI-DING FOR THE LEAD, AND THE

DANCE HALL GALS BE - GIN THE SHOW.

OH BURY ME NOT ON THE LONE PRAIRIE

Oh bury me not on the lone prairie
These words came low and mournfully
From the pallid lips of a youth who lay
On his dying bed at the close of day

He wailed in pain and o'er his brow
Death shadows fast were gathering now
He thought of his home and his loved ones nigh
While the cowboys gathered to see him die

It matters not I've oft been told
Where the body lies when the heart grows cold
But grant oh grant this wish to me
And bury me not on the lone prairie

Oh bury me not on the lone prairie
In a narrow grave, six by three
Where the buffalo paws o'er the prairie sea
Oh bury me not on the lone prairie

Oh bury me not on the lone prairie
Where the wild coyote will howl o'er me
Where the rattlesnake hiss and the crow flies free
Oh bury me not on the lone prairie

Oh bury me not and his voice failed there
But we paid no heed to his dying prayer
In a narrow grave six by three
We buried him there on the lone prairie

Gillette Brothers *"Many Long Miles to Ride"* 2006

Cowboy Songs Old & New

Oh bu-ry me not on the lone prai - rie.

These words came low and mourn - ful - ly.

From the pal - lid lips of a youth who lay

on his dy - ing bed at the close of day.

OH MY DARLING CLEMENTINE

In a cavern, in a canyon
Excavating for a mine
Dwelt a miner, forty-niner
And his daughter Clementine

OH MY DARLING, OH MY DARLING
OH MY DARLING, CLEMENTINE
YOU ARE LOST AND GONE FOREVER
DREADFUL SORRY, CLEMENTINE

Light she was and like a fairy
And her shoes were number nine
Herring boxes without topses
Sandals were for Clementine

Drove she ducklings to the water
Ev'ry morning just at nine
Hit her foot against a splinter
Fell into the foaming brine

Ruby lips above the water
Blowing bubbles soft and fine
But alas I was no swimmer
So I lost my Clementine

Verse: In a ca-vern, in a can-yon, ex-ca-va-ting for a mine, dwelt a mi-ner, for-ty - ni - ner and his daugh - ter Cle-men-tine. OH MY

Chorus: DAR-LING, OH MY DAR-LING, OH MY DAR-LING CLE-MEN-TINE. YOU ARE LOST AND GONE FOR - EV - ER DREAD-FUL SOR-RY CLE-MEN-TINE.

OH SUSANNA

Stephen Foster (1848)

Well I come from Alabama
With my banjo on my knee
Goin' to Louisiana
My true love for to see

OH SUSANNA
DON'T YOU CRY FOR ME
COME FROM ALABAMA WITH
MY BANJO ON MY KNEE

Rained all night the day I left
The weather it was dry
Sun so hot I froze to death
Susanna don't you cry

Had a dream the other night
When everything was still
I dreamed I saw Susanna
Coming down the hill

Gillette Brothers *"Cowboys, Minstrels and Medicine Shows"* 2010

Verse

Well I come from Al - a - ba-ma with my ban-jo on my knee.

Goin' to Lou - si - a - na, my true love for to see.

Chorus

OH SU - SAN-NA, DON'T YOU CRY FOR ME.

COME FROM AL - A - BA-MA WITH MY BAN-JO ON MY KNEE.

THE OLD CHISHOLM TRAIL

Well come on boys
And listen to my tale
I'll tell you of my troubles
On the ol' Chisholm Trail

COME A-TI YI YIPPY
YIPPY YEA YIPPY YEA
COME A-TI YI YIPPY YIPPY YEA

We started up the trail
October twenty-third
Started up the trail
With the TU herd

On a ten-dollar horse
And a forty-dollar saddle
I was headin' down to Texas
For to punch them cattle

With my foot in the stirrup
And my hand on the horn
I'm the best damn cowboy
Ever was born

Well ol' Ben Bolt
Was a fine ol' boss
He went to see his gal
On a sore-backed horse

It's bacon and beans
Most every day
I'd rather be eatin'
That prairie hay

There's a stray in the herd
And the boss said kill it
So I bedded him down
In the bottom of a skillet

I'm up every morning
'Fore daylight
And before I sleep
The moon be shining bright

We're ropin' and a tyin'
And a-brandin' all day
And I'm a-workin' might hard
For mighty little pay

It's cloudy in the west
And lookin' like rain
And my derned old slicker's
In the wagon again

Now my horse threw me off
At a creek called Mud
And my horse threw me off
And I landed with a thud

So I went to the boss
To draw my roll
And he had me figured out
Nine dollars in the hole

I'm goin' to get married
As quick as I can
And I won't punch cattle
For no damn man

We loaded them up
And we put them on the cars
And that was the last
Of the old Two Bars

Gillette Brothers "Many Long Miles to Ride" 2006

Verse

Well come on boys and lis-ten to my tale. I'll

tell you of my trou-bles on the ol' Chis-holm trail. COME A -

Chorus

TI YI YIP - PY YIP - PY YEA YIP - PY YEA, COME A -

TI YI YIP - PY YIP - PY YEA.

OLD DAN TUCKER

Dan Emmett (1843)

I come to town the other night
Heard the crowd, saw the fight
The watchman was a-running 'round
Sayin' Old Dan Tucker's come to town

GET OUT THE WAY
GET OUT THE WAY
GET OUT THE WAY OLD DAN TUCKER
YOU'RE TOO LATE TO COME TO SUPPER

Well Old Dan Tucker was a nice old man
He used to ride on a darby ram
Sent him whizzen down the hill
If he ain't got up he's layin' there still

Well Old Dan Tucker and I got drunk
He fell in the fire and kicked up a chunk
The charcoal went inside his shoe
I'll tell you boys them ashes flew

Well I went to town to buy some goods
I lost myself in a piece of woods
The night was cold and I did suffer
I nearly froze to death me and Old Dan Tucker

Old Dan Tucker went a-ridin' to town
Ridin' a goat and leadin' a hound
The hound did bark and the goat did jump
And Old Dan Tucker went bump on a stump

I come to town the other night
Heard the crowd, saw the fight
The watchman was a-running 'round
Sayin' Old Dan Tucker's come to town

Gillette Brothers *"Cowboys, Minstrels and Medicine Shows"* 2010

Cowboy Songs Old & New

Dan Emmett

Verse

F   C   D m

I come to town the o - ther night, heard the crowd, saw the fight. The

F   C   D m

watch-man was a - run-ning 'round say-in' Old Dan Tuck-er's come to town.

F   C   F

Chorus

GET OUT THE WAY   GET OUT THE WAY

F   C   B♭   C   F

GET OUT THE WAY OLD DAN TUCK-ER, YOU'RE TOO LATE TO COME TO SUP-PER.

THE OVERLANDERS

There's a trade you all know well
It's bringing cattle over
On every track to the Gulf and back
Men know the Queensland drover

SO PASS THE BILLY ROUND BOYS
DON'T YOU LET THE PINT POT STAND THERE
FOR TONIGHT WE DRINK THE HEALTH
OF EVERY OVERLANDER

I come from northern plains
Where the girls and grass are scanty
Where the creeks run dry or ten feet high
And it's either drought or plenty

There are men from every land
From Spain and France and Flanders
They're a well-mixed pack both white and black
The Queensland overlanders

When we've earned a spree in town
We live like pigs in clover
And the whole damn cheque pours down the neck
Of many a Queensland drover

As I pass along the road
The children raise my dander
Shouting mother dear take in the clothes
Here comes an overlander

There's a girl in Sydney Town
Who said please don't leave me lonely
I said it's sad but my old prad
Has room for one man only

But I'm bound for home once more
On a prad that's quite a goer
I can find a job with a crawling mob
On the banks of the Maranoa

Verse

There's a trade you all know well, it's bring-ing cat-tle o-ver. On

ev - ery track to the Gulf and back men know the Queens-land dro-ver. SO

Chorus

PASS THE BIL-LY ROUND BOYS, DON'T LET THE PINT POT STAND THERE. FOR TO-

NIGHT WE DRINK THE HEALTH OF EV - ERY O - VER - LAN-DER.

THE POT WRASTLER

Curley Fletcher

How are you there cowboy I hope you are well
Just light from your saddle and rest for a spell
Here are the makin's so roll you a smoke
You're just out of town and I bet you are broke

You look like ol' hunger been ridin' you hard
Sit down and eat boy you are welcome old pard
I spent a lot of years ridin' the range
But now I am wrasslin' the pots for a change

Now I ain't no chef like ol' Delmonico
But I savvies the mixins' of old sour dough
Sorts all the big rocks right out of the beans
And I don't wipe the fryin' pans off on my jeans

Oh the chuck is all right and the wagon keeps neat
If you don't like my cookin' you don't have to eat
Well I'm the pot wrassler but I ain't no dub
I'm close to my bed boys I'm close to the grub

I'm a little bit old and I don't want no truck
With horn-hookin' cattle or horses that buck
I've rode many a year and my legs is all bowed
I've got to the age where I'm easily throwed

I got the rheumatics, my hands is all burned
My joints is all stiff and my belly's all churned
I'm the pot wrassler you're hearin' me shout
Come on and get it 'fore I throw it out

You fellers rope steers to down 'em and tie 'em
Then I come along to skin 'em and fry 'em
I get forty a month and the cookin' to do
So I guess I'm all through bein' a wild buckaroo

When you punchers is out in the blizzard and storm
I'm close to the fire where I can stay warm
So do your old ridin' you wild galoots
And I'll wrastle the pots you can bet your damn boots

Gillette Brothers *"Home Ranch"* 1992

Curley Fletcher

How are you there cow-boy I hope you are well. Just

light from your sad - dle and rest for a spell.

Here are the ma - kin's so roll you a smoke. You're

just out of town and I bet you are broke.

PUʻU HULUHULU

The rain and the mist are all around me
The never-ending rains of Maʻili
The thoughts of the rough land surround me
And the ghostly silence cuts right through me

Naʻu i lahui i ka leo
ʻIke i ka makani Kaʻieulu
Ka makani o ka ʻaina
I laila hoʻolaʻi na manu

Oh hill with the hair I long to see you
And down toward the old corral the herd will go
You're the landmark that guides us home - Puʻu Huluhulu
Hill with the hair, Hawaiian cowboy loves you so

Ma loko o ka ulu laʻau
E hoʻolohe i ka leo o na manu
Ka leo aʻe i mai ana
Ka ili aʻe ko ala e malama

Then when we see the wild cattle
We'll drive them down to Puʻu Huluhulu
So get your lassos ready for the battle
And if you fall never mind you'll make it through

ʻOʻoe ka i hui i hola
Ka manaʻo e puapuaʻi ala
Eia aʻe ʻo Puʻu Huluhulu
Hulu no wau ia ʻoe, ua hiki no

High up on the peaks of the mountains
Ropin' cattle is what we do
From Maulua over to Puʻoa
Two big mountains but never mind we'll make it through

Hoʻomakaukau kou kaula ʻili
Iluna o ka puʻu Kanakaleonui
E hoʻolohe i ke kani o na manu
Oh never mind, ke hina pu ua, hiki no

Clyde "Kindy" Sproat *"Na Mele O Paniolo (Songs of the Hawaiian Cowboy)"* 1997

Cowboy Songs Old & New

The rain and the mist are all a - round me. The ne - ver
end - ing rains of Ma - i - li. The
thoughts of the rough land sur - round me, and the
ghost - ly si - lence cuts right through me.

THE RAMBLING GAMBLER

I'm a rambler, I'm a gambler
I'm a long way from my home
If the people don't like me
They can leave me alone

Oh it's dark and it's rainin'
And the moon it gives no light
And my pony he won't travel
This dark road at night

I used to have me a pretty little sweetheart
Her age was seventeen
She was the flower of Belton
And the rose of Killeen

But her parents were against me
And now she is the same
If I'm on your books babe
Won't you blot out my name

I'm a rambler, I'm a gambler
I'm a long way from my home
If the people don't like me
They can leave me alone

Oh it's dark and it's rainin'
And the moon it gives no light
And my pony he won't travel
This dark road at night

Gillette Brothers "Lone Star Trail" 1997

I'm a ram-bler, I'm a gam-bler. I'm a long way from my home. If the

peo-ple don't like me, they can leave me a - lone.

THE RED RIVER VALLEY

From this valley they say you are going
I shall miss your sweet face and your smile
Because you are weary and tired
You are changing your range for a while

I've been thinking a long time my darling
Of the sweet words you never would say
Now alas must my fond hopes all vanish
For they say you are going away

COME AND SIT BY MY SIDE E'ER YOU LEAVE ME
DO NOT HASTEN TO BID ME ADIEU
JUST REMEMBER THE RED RIVER VALLEY
AND THE COWBOY WHO LOVES YOU SO TRUE

I have promised you darling that never
Will words from my lips cause you pain
And my life it will be yours forever
If only you will love me again

Must the past with its joys all be blighted
By the future of sorrow and pain
Must the vows that were spoken be slighted
Don't you think you could love me again

There never could be such a longing
In the heart of a poor cowboy's breast
As dwells in the heart you are breaking
As I wait in my home in the West

Do you think of this valley you're leaving
Oh how lonely and dreary it'll be
Do you think of the kind hearts you're hurting
And the pain you are causing to me

Verse

From this val-ley they say you are going. I shall miss your sweet face and your smile. Be-

cause you are wea-ry and ti-red, you are chang-ing your range for a-while. COME AND

Chorus

SIT BY MY SIDE E'ER YOU LEAVE ME. DO NOT HAS-TEN TO BID ME A-DIEU. JUST RE-

MEM-BER THE RED RI-VER VAL-LEY AND THE COW-BOY WHO LOVES YOU SO TRUE.

RED WING

Thurland Chattaway / Kerry Mills (1907)

There once lived an Indian maid
A shy little prairie maid
Who sang a lay, a love song gay
As on the plains she'd while away the day
She loved a warrior bold
This shy little maid of old
But brave and gay he rode one day
To battle far away

NOW THE MOON SHINES TONIGHT
ON PRETTY RED WING
THE BREEZE IS SIGHING
THE NIGHT BIRD'S CRYING
FOR AFAR 'NEATH HIS STAR
HER BRAVE IS SLEEPING
WHILE RED WING'S WEEPING
HER HEART AWAY

She watched for him day and night
She kept all the campfires bright
And under the sky each night she would lie
And dream about his coming by and by
But when all the braves returned
The heart of Red Wing yearned
For far, far away her warrior gay
Fell bravely in the fray

.

Thurland Chattaway / Kerry Mills (1907)

Verse

There once lived an Ind – ian maid, a shy lit – tle prai – rie maid, who
sang a lay a love song gay as on the plains whe'd while a – way the day. She
loved a an war – rior bold, this shy lit – tle maid of old, but
brave and gay he rode one day to bat – tle far a – way. NOW THE

Chorus

MOON SHINES TO – NIGHT ON PRET – TY RED WING. THE BREEZE IS
SIGH – ING THE NIGHT BIRD'S CRY – ING. FOR A –
FAR 'NEATH HIS STAR HER BRAVE IS SLEEP – ING WHILE RED WING'S
WEEP – ING HER HEART A – WAY.

ROUNDUP IN THE SPRING

In the lobby of a big hotel in New York Town one day
Sat a bunch of fellows telling yarns to pass the time away
They talked of places that they'd been and different sights they'd seen
Some of them praised Chicago Town and others New Orleans

In a corner in a big armchair sat a man whose hair was gray
He listened to them eagerly to what they had to say
They asked him where he'd like to be his clear old voice did ring
I'd like to be in Texas for the roundup in the spring

I CAN SEE THE CATTLE GRAZING O'ER THE HILLS OF EARLY MORN
I CAN SEE THE CAMPFIRES SMOKING AT THE BREAKING OF THE DAWN
I CAN HEAR THE BRONCO'S NEIGHING, HEAR THE COWBOY SING
I'D LIKE TO BE IN TEXAS FOR THE ROUNDUP IN THE SPRING

Well they all sat still and listened to every word he had to say
They knew the old man sitting there had been a top hand in his day
They asked him for a story of his life out on the range
Slowly he removed his hat and quietly began

Well I've seen 'em stampede o'er the hills till you'd think they'd never stop
I've seen 'em run for miles and miles until their leaders dropped
I was foreman of a cow ranch, the calling of a king
Well I'd like to be in Texas for the roundup in the spring

Well there's a grave in sunny Texas where Josie Bidwell sleeps
There's a grove of leafy cottonwoods her constant vigil keeps
In my mind's recollection of the long long bygone days
We rode the range together like two skippin' kids at play

Her gentle voice it calls me in the watches of the night
I hear her laughter freshening the dew of early light
I was foreman of a cow ranch, the calling of a king
Well I'd like to be in Texas for the roundup in the spring

Gillette Brothers *"Cowboys, Minstrels and Medicine Shows"* 2010

Cowboy Songs Old & New

Verse

In the lob-by of a big ho-tel in New York Town one day, sat a

bunch of fel-lows tel-ling yarns to pass the time a-way. They

talked of pla-ces that they'd been and dif-ferent sights they'd seen.

Some of them praised Chi-ca-go town and o-thers New Or-leans. I CAN

Chorus

SEE THE CAT-TLE GRA-ZING O'ER THE HILL OF EAR-LY MORN. I CAN

SEE THE CAMP-FIRES SMO-KING AT THE BREA-KING OF THE DAWN. I CAN

HEAR THE BRON-CO'S NEIGH-ING, HEAR THE COW-BOY SING. OH I'D

LIKE TO BE IN TEX-AS FOR THE ROUND-UP IN THE SPRING.

RYE WHISKEY

I'll eat when I'm hungry
I'll drink when I'm dry
If the hard times don't kill me
I'll lay down and die

RYE WHISKEY, RYE WHISKEY
RYE WHISKEY, I CRY
IF YOU DON'T GIVE ME RYE WHISKEY
I SURELY WILL DIE

I'll tune up my fiddle
And I'll rosin my bow
I'll make myself welcome
Wherever I go

Beefsteak when I'm hungry
Red liquor when I'm dry
Greenbacks when I'm hard up
And religion when I die

They say I drink whiskey
My money's my own
All them that don't like me
Can leave me alone

Sometimes I drink whiskey
Sometimes I drink rum
Sometimes I drink brandy
At other times none

But if I get boozy
My whiskey's my own
And them that don't like me
Can leave me alone

Jack o' diamonds, Jack o' diamonds
I know you of old
You've robbed my poor pockets
Of silver and gold

Oh whiskey you villain
You've been my downfall
You've kicked me you've cuffed me
But I love you for all

If the ocean was whiskey
And I was a duck

I'd dive to the bottom
To get one sweet suck

But the ocean ain't whiskey
And I ain't a duck
So we'll round up the cattle
And then we'll get drunk

My foot's in my stirrup
My bridle's in my hand
I'm leaving sweet Lillie
The fairest in the land

Her parents don't like me
They say I'm too poor
They say I'm unworthy
To enter her door

Sweet milk when I'm hungry
Rye whiskey when I'm dry
If a tree don't fall on me
I'll live till I die

I'll buy my own whiskey
I'll make my own stew
If I get drunk, madam
It's nothing to you

I'll drink my own whiskey
I'll drink my own wine
Some ten thousand bottles
I've killed in my time

I've no wife to quarrel
No babies to bawl
The best way of living
Is no wife at all

Way up on Clinch Mountain
I wander alone
I'm as drunk as the devil
Oh let me alone

You may boast of your knowledge
An' brag of your sense
'Twill all be forgotten
A hundred years hence

Verse

G   D

I'll eat when I'm hun-gry I'll drink when I'm dry. If the

G   C   G

hard times don't kill me I'll lay down and die. RYE

Chorus

G   C   G

WHIS-KEY, RYE WHIS-KEY, RYE WHIS-KEY, I CRY. IF YOU

G   C   G

DON'T GIVE ME RYE WHIS-KEY I SURE-LY WILL DIE.

SAM BASS

Sam Bass was born in Indiana
It was his native home
And at the age of seventeen
Young Sam began to roam
He first came out to Texas
A cowboy for to be
A kinder-hearted fellow
You'll seldom ever see

Sam used to deal in race stock
One called the Denton mare
He matched her in scrub races
And took her to the fair
Sam used to coin the money
And spent it just as free
He always drank good whiskey
Wherever he might be

Sam left the Collins ranch
In the merry month of May
With a herd of Texas cattle
The Black Hills for to see
Sold out in Custer City
And then got on a spree
A harder set of cowboys
You'll seldom ever see

On their way back to Texas
They robbed the U.P. train
Then split up into couples
And started out again
Joe Collins and his partner
Were overtaken soon
With all their hard-earned money
They had to meet their doom

Sam met his fate at Round Rock
July the twenty-first
They pierced poor Sam with rifle balls
And emptied out his purse
Poor Sam he is a corpse now
And six feet under clay
While Jackson's in the bushes
Trying to get away

Jim had borrowed Sam's good gold
And didn't want to pay
The only shot he saw
Was to give poor Sam away
He sold out Sam and Barnes
And left their friends to mourn
Oh what a scorching Jim will get
When Gabriel blows his horn

He sold out Sam and Barnes
And left their friends to mourn
Oh what a scorching Jim will get
When Gabriel blows his horn
Perhaps he's gone to heaven
There's none of us can say
But if I'm right in my surmise
He's gone the other way

Gillette Brothers "Lone Star Trail" 1997

Sam Bass was born in Ind - i - an - a it was his na - tive home. And

at the age of se - ven - teen Young Sam be - gan to roam. He

first came out to Tex - as, a cow - boy for to be. A

kin - der heart - ted fel - low you'll sel - dom ev - er see.

THE SANTA FE TRAIL

James Grafton Rogers (1911)

Tell me friend have you sighted a schooner
Alongside of the Santa Fe Trail
And it made it here Monday or sooner
Had a water keg tied to its tail
There was a Pa and a Ma on the mule-seat
But somewheres along by the way
Was a tow-headed gal on a pinto
Just a-jangling for old Santa Fe

YO-HO, YO-HO
JUST A-JANGLING FOR OLD SANTA FE

I seen them ride down the arroyo
As they crossed on them Arkansas sand
She had smiles like acres of sunflowers
Held a quirt in her little brown hand
Well she mounted her pinto so airy
And she rode like she carried the mail
And her eyes near set fire to the prairie
Alongside of the Santa Fe Trail

Well I once knew a gal on the border
Who I'd ride to El Paso to sight
I have danced in some high-steppin' order
And I've sometimes kissed some girls goodnight
But Lord they're all ruffles and beading
And they drink fancy tea by the pail
I'm not used to that kind of stampeding
Alongside of the Santa Fe Trail

Well I don't know her name on the prairie
When you are hunting one girl it's so wide
And it's shorter from hell to hilary
Than it is on that Santa Fe ride
But I'll try and reach Plummers by sundown
Where a camp can be made in the swale
Then I'll come upon that gal with her pinto
Alongside of the Santa Fe Trail

Peter Bellamy *"Fair Annie: English, Irish, Australian and American Traditional Songs"* 1983

Cowboy Songs Old & New

Verse

Tell me friend have you sighted a schoo-ner   a-long-side of the San-ta Fe Trail.   And it

made it here Mon-day or soo-ner,   had a wa-ter keg tied to its tail.   There was

Pa and a Ma on the mule-seat,   but some-wheres a-long by the way,   was a

tow-head-ed gal on a pin-to,   just a-jang-ling for old San-ta Fe.   YO-

Chorus

HO,   YO-HO,   JUST A JANG-LING FOR OLD SAN-TA FE.

SENTIMENT TOAST

Waddie Mitchell / Pipp Gillette

Here's to the trail we decided to ride
To the code that we chose to adhere to
To our sunburnt old hide
And our damn foolish pride
And the mischief we seem to get into

Here's to the wages we spend free in town
To the greenhorns with gumption and try
To those friends we have found
Who will not let us down
And the pleasures we cannot deny

Here's to the horses, the cattle, the range
To the drink that is longer and wetter
To those think us strange
Our refusal to change
And the women we'd like to know better

Here's to the trail we decided to ride
To the code that we chose to adhere to
To our sunburnt old hide
And our damn foolish pride
And the mischief we seem to get into

Pipp Gillette *"Singing Songs with Waddie & Pipp"* 2015

Cowboy Songs Old & New

Waddie Mitchell, Pipp Gillette

Here's to the trail we de - ci - ded to ride. To the

code that we chose to ad - here to. To our

sun - burnt old hide and our damn fool - ish pride. And the

mis - chief we seem to get in - to.

THE STRAWBERRY ROAN

Curley Fletcher (1915)

I was hangin' round town just a-spending me time
Out of a job and not makin' a dime
When a feller steps up and he said I suppose
You're a bronc rider by the look of your clothes

Well he guesses me right and a good one I claim
I asked him if he had any bad un's to tame
He said I've a bad one that really can buck
And throwing all cowboys he's having great luck

Well I gets real excited I asked what he'd pay
If I'd ride that pony a couple of days
He said ten bucks and I said I'm your man
I've never seen a pony that I couldn't fan

Stayed until mornin' and right after chuck
I go down to see if that pony could buck
There in the horse corral standing alone
Was a little old caballo a strawberry roan

His legs were all spavined he had pigeon toes
Little pig eyes and a big Roman nose
Little short ears that were split at the tips
And a map of Chihuahua all over his hips

He was u-necked an old, had a big lower jaw
You could tell with one eye he was a regular outlaw
I buckled on me spurs, was sure feelin' fine
Pulled down me old hat and I gathered me twine

Piled the rope on him and boys I knew then
Before he gets rode well I'll sure earn me ten
First come the blind, oh say what a fight
Next come the old saddle I screwed 'er down tight

I crawled to his middle and I lifted the blind
Get out of the way boy and let him unwind
He went a broad walk then he heaved a great sigh
He only lacked wings for to be on the fly

Turned that old belly right up to the sun
You old sunfishin', you son of a gun
He was the worst bucker I've seen on the range
He could turn on a nickel and give you your change

Go up in the air or around on his side
I don't see what kept him from losing his hide
Losin' me stirrups and also my hat
Gone for leather as blind as a bat

Then all of a sudden he went up on high
He left me a sittin' way up in the sky
Turned over twice I come back to earth
I sit there a-cussin' the day of his birth

There's ponies right there I ain't able to ride
There's one of 'em left boys they ain't all died
I'll bet my money there's no man alive
That can ride Old Strawberry
When he takes that high dive

Wilf Carter *"Dynamite Trail/The Strawberry Roan"* 1955

Cowboy Songs Old & New

I was hang - in' round town just a - spend - ing me time,

out of a job and not ma - kin' a dime. When a

fel - ler steps up and he said I sup - pose,

you're a bronc ri - der by the look of your clothes.

THE STREETS OF LAREDO

As I walked out in the streets of Laredo
As I walked out in Laredo one day
I spied a young cowboy wrapped all in white linen
Wrapped in white linen as cold as the clay

OH BEAT THE DRUM SLOWLY
AND PLAY THE FIFE LOWLY
SING THE DEATH MARCH
AS YOU CARRY ME ALONG
TAKE ME TO THE VALLEY
THERE LAY THE SOD O'ER ME
I'M A YOUNG COWBOY
AND KNOW I'VE DONE WRONG

I see by your outfit that you are a cowboy
These words he did say as I boldly walked by
Come sit down beside me and hear my sad story
Got shot in the breast and I know I must die

Go fetch me some water, a cool cup of water
To cool my parched lips then the poor cowboy said
Before I returned his spirit had left him
Had gone to his Maker, the cowboy was dead

Marty Robbins *"More Gunfighter Ballads and Trail Songs"* 1960

Cowboy Songs Old & New

Verse & Chorus

As I walked out in the streets of La - re - do, As
OH BEAT THE DRUM SLOW-LY AND PLAY THE FIFE LOW-LY AND

I walked out in La - re - do one day, I
SING THE DEATH MARCH AS YOU CARRY ME A - LONG. TAKE

spied a young cow - boy wrapped all in white li - nen,
ME TO THE VAL - LEY THERE LAY THE SOD O'ER ME

wrapped in white li - nen as cold as the clay.
I'M A YOUNG COW - BOY AND KNOW I'VE DONE WRONG.

SWEET BETSY FROM PIKE

John A. Stone (1858)

Have you heard tell of sweet Betsy from Pike
She crossed the wide prairie with her lover Ike
With two yoke of oxen, a big yellow dog
A tall Shanghai rooster and one spotted hog

One evening quite early they camped on the Platte
'Twas nearby the road on a green shady flat
Where Betsy, sore-footed, lay down to repose
And in wonder Ike gazed on his Pike County rose

The Injuns came down in a wild yelling horde
And Betsy got scared they would scalp her adored
So under the wagon wheel Betsy did crawl
She fought off them Injuns with musket and ball

It was out on the prairie one dark stormy night
They broke out the whiskey and Betsy got tight
She sang and she shouted she danced on the plain
She made a great show for the whole wagon train

The Shanghai ran off and the cattle all died
The last piece of bacon that morning was fried
Ike was discouraged and Betsy got mad
The dog wagged his tail and looked wondrously sad

They soon reached the desert where Betsy gave out
And down in the sand she lay rolling about
While Ike in great terror looked on in surprise
Saying Betsy get up you'll get sand in your eyes

Sweet Betsy got up in a great deal of pain
Declared she'd go back to Pike County again
Ike heaved a sigh and they fondly embraced
And she traveled along with her arm 'round his waist

Connie Dover *"The Border of Heaven"* 2001

John A. Stone

Have you heard tell of sweet Bet - sy from Pike? She crossed the wide prai - rie with her lo - ver Ike. With two yoke of ox - en, a big yel - low dog, a tall Shang - hai roo - ster and one spot - ted hog.

TEN THOUSAND CATTLE STRAYING

Owen Wister (1904)

Ten thousand cattle gone astray
Left my range and traveled away
And the sons of guns I'm here to say
Have left me dead broke today

IN GAMBLING HELLS DELAYING
TEN THOUSAND CATTLE STRAYING

And now my gal she's gone, gone away
Left my shack and travelled away
With a son of a gun from I-o-way
And left me a lone man today

She was awful sweet and I loved her so
But that I-o-way feller well he made her go
Now my heart is broke, feelin' mighty low
Drink my life away is all I know

Gillette Brothers "Home Ranch" 1992

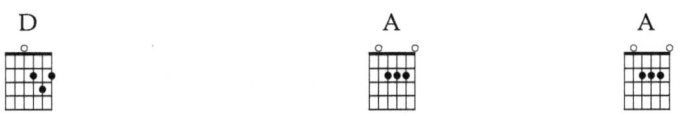

Owen Wister

Verse

Ten thou-sand cat-tle gone a-stray, left my range and tra-veled a-way. And the sons of

guns, I'm here to say, have left me dead broke to-day. IN

Chorus

GAMB-LING HELLS DE-LAY-ING, TEN THOU-SAND CAT-TLE STRAY-ING.

THE TEXAS COWBOY

Mrs. Robt Thomson (1886)

I am a Texas Cowboy
Light hearted gay and free
To roam the wide wide prairie
Is always joy to me ·
My trusty little pony
Is my companion true
O'er plain thro' woods and river
He's sure to pull me thro'

I AM A JOLLY COWBOY
FROM TEXAS NOW I HAIL
GIVE ME MY QUIRT AND PONY
I'M READY FOR THE TRAIL
I LOVE THE ROLLING PRAIRIE
WE'RE FREE FROM CARE AND STRIFE
BEHIND A HERD OF LONGHORNS
I'LL JOURNEY ALL MY LIFE

The early dawn is breaking
Up, up we must away
We vault in to our saddles
And round up then all day
We rope and brand and ear-mark
I tell you we are smart
We get the herd all ready
For Kansas then we start

When low'ring clouds do gather
And lurid lightnings flash
The crashing thunders rattle
And heavy raindrops splash
What keeps the herd from running
And stampede far and wide
The cowboy's long low whistle
And singing by their side

And when in Kansas City
The Boss he pays us up
We loaf around a few days
Then have a parting cup
We bid farewell to city
From noisy marts we come
Right back to dear old Texas
The cowboy's native home

Verse

I am a Tex-as cow-boy, light hearted gay and free. To roam the wide wide prai-rie is al-ways joy to me. My trus-ty lit-tle po-ny is my com-pan-ion true, o'er plain through woods and ri-ver he's sure to pull me thro'. I

Chorus

AM A JOL-LY COW-BOY FROM TEX-AS NOW I HAIL. GIVE ME MY QUIRT AND PO-NY, I'M REA-DY FOR THE TRAIL. I LOVE THE ROL-LING PRAI-RIE, WE'RE FREE FROM CARE AND STRIFE. BE-HIND A HERD OF LONG-HORNS I'LL JOUR-NEY ALL MY LIFE.

TEXIAN BOYS

Oh Louisiana gals come and listen to my noise
Don't go out with Texian boys
If you do your ration it will be
Johnny cake and venison and sassafras tea
Johnny cake and venison and sassafras tea

Now when they go a-courtin' let me tell you what they wear
An old leather coat all picked and bare
An old straw hat more brim than crown
A pair of dirty socks they've worn year 'round
A pair of dirty socks they've worn year 'round

Now when they go a-preachin' let me tell you what they ride
An old pack-saddle all covered with hide
An old hair girth made out of a rope
A-straddle of a horse that can't fetch a lope
A-straddle of a horse that can't fetch a lope

For your wedding supper there's beef and cornbread
There it is to eat when the ceremony's said
When you go to milk you'll milk in a gourd
Set it in the corner and cover it with a board
Set it in the corner and cover it with a board

You'll live in a hut with a hewed log wall
It ain't got any windows at all
With a clapboard roof and a puncheon floor
And that is the way all Texas o'er
That is the way all Texas o'er

Now brandy is brandy any way you mix it
A Texian's a Texian any way you fix him
When other good folk are home in bed
The devil is a-workin' in a Texian's head
The devil is a-workin' in a Texian's head

John Lomax, Jr. *"Sings American Folksongs"* 1956

Cowboy Songs Old & New

Oh Loui - si - an - a gals come and lis - ten to my noise.

Don't go out with Tex - i - an boys.

If you do your ra - tion it will be,

John - ny cake and ven - i - son and sas - sa - fras tea.

John - ny cake and ven - i - son and sas - sa - fras tea.

THE TRAIL TO MEXICO

I made up my mind to change my ways
And quit my crowd that was so gay
To leave my native home for a while
And travel out West for many a mile

It was in the year of eighty-three
That A.J. Stinson hired me
He said young fellow I want you to go
And follow my herd to Mexico

Well it was early in the year
That I went on the trail to drive them steers
I stood my guard in the sleet and the snow
While on the trail to Mexico

Well it was a long and lonesome go
As the herd rolled on to Mexico
With laughter light and the cowboy's song
To Mexico we rolled along

When we arrived in Mexico
I wanted to see my love but I couldn't go
So I wrote a letter, a letter to my dear
But not a word from her did I hear

When I got back to my once-loved home
I called for my darling I thought my own
They said she'd married a richer life
Therefore wild cowboy seek another wife

Oh the girl she's married I do adore
I cannot stay at home anymore
I'll make my way to some foreign land
Or I'll go back to that cowboy band

Oh buddy, oh buddy please don't leave home
Please don't be in a hurry to roam
There's plenty of girls more true than I
Oh don't go West where the bullets fly

It's curse your gold and your silver too
God pity a girl that don't prove true
I'll go out West where the bullets fly
And I'll follow the cow trail until I die

I'll take my bridle in my hand
And I'll go join that cowboy band
I'll bid farewell to the Alamo
And head my horse to Mexico

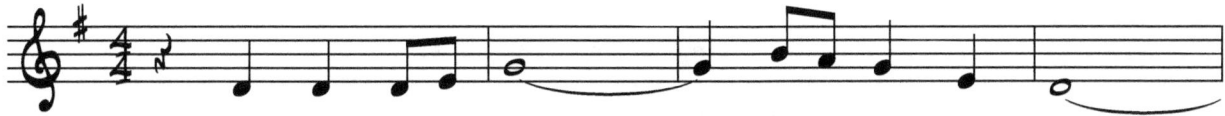

I made up my mind to change my ways,

and quit my crowd that was so gay,

to leave my na - - - tive home for a - while,

and tra-vel out West for ma-ny a mile.

WHEN THE MORNING COMES

Charles Albert Tindley (1905)

We are often tossed and driven on the restless sea of time
Rollin' clouds and howlin' tempests oft succeed the bright sunshine
That land of perfect day when the mist has rolled away
We will understand it better by and by

BY AND BY OH WHEN THE MORNING COMES
ALL THE SAINTS OF GOD ARE GATHERING HOME
WE'LL TELL THE STORY HOW THEY OVERCOME
AND WE'LL UNDERSTAND IT BETTER BY AND BY

Trials dark on every hand but we cannot understand
All the ways that God will lead us to that blessed promised land
He will guide us with his eye, and we'll follow 'till we die
And we'll understand it better by and by

We are often destitute of the things that life demands
Want of shelter and of food, thirsty hill and barren land
But we're trusting in the Lord and according to His word
We will understand it better by and by

Oft our cherished plans have failed, disappointments have prevailed
And we've wandered in the darkness heavyhearted and alone
But we're trusting in the Lord and according to His word
We will understand it better by and by

Temptations, hidden snares often take us unawares
And our hearts are made to bleed for some thoughtless word or deed
And we wonder why the test when we try to do our best
But we'll understand it by and by

Gillette Brothers *"Lone Star Trail"* 1997

Verse

We are of-ten tossed and dr-ven on the rest-less sea of time. Rol-lin'

clouds and how-lin' tem-pests oft suc-ceed the bright sun-shine. That

Chorus

land of per-fect day when the mist has rolled a-way. We will un-der-stand it bet-ter by and by.

BY AND BY OH WHEN THE MOR-NING COMES. ALL THE SAINTS OF GOD ARE GATH-ER-ING HOME.

TELL THE STO-RY HOW THEY O-VER-COME AND WE'LL UN-DER-STAND IT BET-TER BY AND BY.

WHEN THE WORK'S ALL DONE THIS FALL

D.J. O'Malley (1886)

A group of jolly cowboys discussing plans at ease
Says one I'll tell you something if you will listen please
I am an old cowpuncher and here I'm dressed in rags
And I used to be a tough one and take on great big jags

But I have got a home, boys, a good one you all know
Although I have not seen it since long, long ago
I'm going back home, boys, once more to see them all
Yes, I'm going to see my mother when the work's all done this fall

When I left home, boys, my mother for me cried
Begged me not to go, boys, for me she would have died
My mother's heart is breaking, breaking for me that's all
And with Gods help I'll see her when the work's all done this fall

That very night this cowboy went out to stand his guard
The night was dark and cloudy and storming very hard
The cattle they got frightened and rushed in wild stampede
The cowboy tried to head them riding at full speed

While riding in the darkness so loudly he did shout
Trying his best to beat them and turn the herd about
His saddle horse did stumble and on him did fall
The poor boy won't see his mother when the work's all done this fall

They picked him up so gently and laid him on a bed
His body was so mangled the boys all thought him dead
He opened wide his blue eyes and looking all around
He motioned to his comrades to sit near him on the ground

Boys send my mother my wages, the wages I have earned
For I am afraid boys my last steer I have turned
I am headed for a new range, I hear my Master call
And I'll not see my mother when the work's all done this fall

Fred you take my saddle, George you take my bed
Bill you take my pistol after I am dead
And think upon me kindly when you look upon them all
For I'll not see my mother when the work's all done this fall

Charlie was buried at sunrise, no tombstone at his head
Nothing but a little board and this is what it said
Charlie died at daybreak, he died from a fall
And he'll not see his mother when the work's all done this fall

A group of jol-ly cow-boys dis-cus-sing plans at ease, says

one I'll tell you some-thing if you will lis-ten please. I

am an old cow-punch-er and here I'm dressed in rags, and I

used to be a tough one and take on great big jags.

WINDY BILL

Bill was a Texas lad
And he could rope you bet
He said the steer he couldn't tie
He hadn't found him yet
But the boys knew of an old black steer
Sort of an old outlaw
That ran down in the bushes
At the foot of a rocky draw

That old black steer had stood his ground
With punchers everywhere
The boys bet Bill ten to one
He couldn't quite get there
So Bill brought out his old gray horse
His withers and back were raw
And prepared to tackle that big black steer
That ran down in the draw

With his Brazos bit and his Sam Stack tree
And chaps and taps to boot
With his old maguey tied hard and fast
He swore he'd get that brute
When Bill first came a-ridin' down
Old Blackie began to paw
Then he heist his tail up in the air
Went driftin' down the draw

That old gray horse took after him
For he'd been eatin' corn
Bill he piled his old maguey
Right around old Blackie's horns
The old gray horse he stopped right still
And the cinches broke like straw
Billy and the Sam Stack tree
Went driftin' down the draw

Bill lit in a flint rock pile
His face and hands was scratched
He said he thought he could rope a snake
But he guessed he'd met his match
Bill got up and paid his bets
Without a bit of jaw
And allowed he guessed old Blackie's the boss
Of anything in the draw

Now the moral of my story boys
And this you all must see
When you go to rope a steer
Don't tie 'em to your tree
Just take your dally welters
Accordin' to California law
And you won't see your Sam Stack tree
Go driftin' down the draw

Gillette Brothers "Cinch Up Your Riggin'" 1994

Bill was a Tex - as lad and he could rope you bet. He
said the steer he could-n't tie he had - n't found him yet. But the
boys knew of an old black steer sort of an old out - law, that
ran down in the bush - es at the foot of a rock - y draw.

THE YELLOW ROSE OF TEXAS

There's a yellow rose in Texas that I am going to see
No other cowboy knows her, no cowboy only me
She cried so when I left her, it like to broke my heart
And if I ever find her we never more will part

SHE'S THE SWEETEST ROSE OF COLOR
THIS COWBOY EVER KNEW
HER EYES ARE BRIGHT AS DIAMONDS
THEY SPARKLE LIKE THE DEW
YOU MAY TALK ABOUT YOUR DEAREST MAY
AND SING OF ROSA LEE
BUT THE YELLOW ROSE OF TEXAS
IS THE ONLY GAL FOR ME

Where the Rio Grande is flowing and the starry skies are bright
She walks along the river in the quiet summer night
She thinks if I remember when we parted long ago
I promised to come back again and not to leave her so

Oh now I'm going to find her for my heart is full of woe
And we'll sing the song together that we sung so long ago
We'll play the banjo gaily and we'll sing the songs of yore
And the Yellow Rose of Texas shall be mine forevermore

Verse

There's a yel-low rose in Tex-as that I am going to see. No
o-ther cow-boy knows her, no cow-boy on-ly me. She
cried so when I left her, it like to broke my heart. And
if I ev-er find her we ne-ver more will part. SHE'S THE

Chorus

SWEET-EST ROSE OF CO-LOR THIS COW-BOY EV-ER KNEW. HER
EYES ARE BRIGHT AS DIA-MONDS, THEY SPAR-KLE LIKE THE DEW. YOU MAY
TALK A-BOUT YOUR DEAR-EST MAY AND SING OF RO-SA LEE, BUT THE
YEL-LOW ROSE OF TEX-AS IS THE ON-LY GAL FOR ME.

THE ZEBRA DUN

We was camped out on the plains
At the head of the Cimarron
Along comes a stranger
And he stopped to argue some
He looked so very foolish
And began to look around
We thought he was a greenhorn
Just escaped from town

We asked if he'd had breakfast
And he had not had a sniff
We opened up the chuckbox
And told him help his self
He took a little beefsteak
A biscuit and some beans
And he then begun to talk about
The foreign kings and queens

He talked about the Spanish War
And fightin' on the seas
With guns as big as beef steers
And ramrods big as trees
And he talked about ol' Paul Jones
A fightin' son of a gun
And he said he was the grittiest cuss
That ever pulled a gun

Such an educated feller
His thoughts just come in herds
He astonished all us punchers
With his jaw breakin' words
He just kept right on talkin'
Till he made the boys all sick
And we began to look around
For how to play a trick

He said he'd lost his job
Out upon the Santa Fe
He was goin' across the plains
For to strike the Seven D
But he didn't say how come it
Just some trouble with his boss
He said he'd like to borrow
A nice fat saddle horse

This tickled all the boys to death
We laughed down in our sleeves
Said that he could have a horse
As fresh as he would please
So Shorty grabbed the lasso
And he roped the Zebra Dun
And led him to the stranger
As we waited for the fun

Now old Dun he was an outlaw
He had grown so awful wild
He could paw the white out of
the moon
And he could jump for a mile
And he always stood right still
'Twas like he didn't know
Until he were saddled
And a-ready for to go

Now the stranger hit the saddle
And old Dun he quit the earth
And went straight up in the air
For all that he was worth
A-balllin' and a-squawlin'
And a-having a wall-eyed fit
With his hind feet perpendicular
And his front ones in the bits

Now we could see the tops of trees
In this and every jump
The stranger he was growed there
Just like a camel's hump
And he sat up there upon him
And he twirled his black moustache
Just like a summer boarder
A-waitin' for his hash

Now he thumped him in the shoulders
And he spurred him when he whirled
He showed us flunky punchers
He's the wolf of this ol' world
And when he had dismounted
Once again upon the ground
Why we knew he was a thoroughbred
And not a juke from town

Now the boss he was a-standin'
An' a-watchin' all the show
He walked right up to him
And he asked him not to go
If you can use a lasso
Like you rode the Zebra Dun
The you're the man I've looked for
Ever since the Year of One

Well he could use a lasso
And he didn't do it slow
The cattle they stampeded
He was always on the go
A one thing and a sure thing
That I've learned since I was born
Every educated feller
He ain't a plumb greenhorn

Don Edwards "Saddle Songs" 1997

We was camped out on the plains at the head of the Ci-mar-ron. A-

long comes a stran-ger and he stopped to ar - gue some. He

looked so ve - ry fool - ish and be - gan to look a-round. We

thought he was a green-horn and just es-caped from town.

Cowboy Songs Old & New

SONG NOTES

After the Chores

A banjo tune by Pipp Gillette, written while relaxing on his front porch after a hard day's work on his ranch in Texas. Transposed here from the key of F to the key of C.

Ain't No More Cane on the Brazos

This prison work song was collected by John Lomax from Central State Farm in Texas.

At the End of the Santa Fe Trail

A new song written by Bernard Wrigley from Lancashire, England, and inspired by an article in National Geographic.

The Ballad of Jesse James

Jesse James was killed by fellow outlaw gang member Robert Ford in St. Joseph, Missouri, in April 1882 and this 19th century folk song was first recorded by Bentley Ball in 1919.

Been All Around This World

The outlaw in this song might very well have been hanged in Fort Smith, Arkansas, by Hangin' Judge Parker in the 1870's.

Billy the Kid

Born Henry McCarty in 1859 and known as William H. Bonney, "Billy the Kid" became a well-known gunfighter, outlaw and cattle rustler who was gunned down at the age of 21 by Sheriff Pat Garrett in New Mexico in 1881.

Billy Vanero

Derived from "The Ride of Paul Venerez" written by Eben E. Rexford in 1881. Rexford also wrote "Silver Threads Among the Gold".

Bravest Cowboy

An oldtime song collected from Tommy Jarrell of Mt Airy, North Carolina, and learned from the concertina playing of Jody Kruskal.

The Brazos River Song

Also known as "The Rivers of Texas" this song was first collected in Arkansas from Mrs. Irene Carlisle and names many of the major rivers in Texas.

Bucking Bronco

Attributed by some to Belle Starr c.1878, which is very possible considering the sexual innuendo still in this song, even with the cleaned-up lyrics.

Buffalo Gal

Published in 1844 by blackface minstrel John Hodges as "Lubly Fan" and as "Buffalo Gals" in 1848 about the women in Buffalo, New York.

The Chuckwagon's Mired

First published in 1914 by E.A. Brininstool as "Trouble for the Range Cook". A "riata" is a lariat or lasso usually made of braided fibers from the Mexican maguey plant. A "waddie" was originally a rustler or thief but has since become another word for cowboy.

Cielito Lindo

A favorite of Mexican mariachi bands, it was written in 1882 by Quirino Mendoza y Cortés. A term of endearment, "Cielito" means "little sky" or "little heaven" and "Lindo" translates to "cute", "pretty" and also "lovely".

Cocinero

A new song by Fran Hedrick and Pipp Gillette. "Cocinero" is the Spanish word for a cook.

The Colorado Trail

Carl Sandburg collected this traditional song from Dr. T.L. Chapman of Duluth, Minnesota, who had learned it decades earlier from a badly broken cowboy patient.

Cowboy Jack

A variation of "Your Mother Prays for You, Jack" (1893) it is likely this cowboy version comes from Arizona.

The Cowboy Life

First published in 1908, this song is a cowboy adaptation of a lumberjack ballad which in turn was an adaptation of the old English sailor's song "The Shantyman's Life".

Cowboy's Dream

According to John Lomax this was composed in 1873 by Charley Hart, calling it "Drift to That Sweet By-and-By" and later set to the tune "My Bonny Lies Over the Ocean".

The Cowman's Prayer

First published by Jack Thorp in 1908 as heard in a cow camp near Fort Sumner, New Mexico on the Pecos River.

Curley Joe

Learned by the Gillette Brothers from Montana singer Duane Dickinson. The song dates at least to the early 1920's. "Forked" is pronounced "fork-ed" and means to ride a bronc well.

The Devil Made Texas

Also known as "Hell in Texas" and usually sung to the tune "The Irish Washerwoman". It was printed on a broadside as early as 1909 and freely distributed by the proprietor of the Buckhorn Saloon in San Antonio.

Diamond Joe

There are at least three different songs with this title. This one was collected by John Lomax from J.D. Dillingham who learned it in the 1870's in central Texas.

Doney Gal

The word "doney" comes from the Spanish word "doña" and means "sweetheart". In this instance it refers to the cowboy's horse.

Down in the Valley

First published in 1909, the song is also sometimes called "Birmingham Jail".

The Dreary Black Hills

Collected by John Lomax in *Cowboy Songs and Other Frontier Ballads*, it dates to c.1885 and refers to the Black Hills in the Badlands of South Dakota.

Git Along Little Dogies

First notated in Owen Wister's western diary in 1893. Wister would later become famous for writing *The Virginian*. A dogie is a motherless or neglected calf.

Goin' to the West

An old folk song from the mountains of Northern Alabama dating to c.1880.

The Gouge-Eye Saloon

Written by East Texas oldtime musician Steve Hartz in 2003 for performances of the Atoyac Valley Medicine Show, inspired by an infamous backwoods tavern on a high bluff that overlooked the Neches River.

The Great Western Woods

Written by Steve Hartz and featured in his hardbound book and audio CD *Settlers of the Western Woods* (2012). When East Texas riverboat captain Andrew Smyth wrote a letter home to his folks in Alabama he used "The Great Western Woods" as his return address.

Green Grow the Lilacs

Also known as "Green Grow the Laurels" and dating to at least 1846. Some have said the term "gringo" comes from this song, but the word is in a 1787 Spanish dictionary.

The High-Toned Dance

Written by James Barton Adams, this song first appeared in John Lomax's *Songs of the Cattle Trail and Cow Camp* published in 1919.

Home on the Range

"My Western Home" was a poem written in 1872 by Dr. Brewster Higley with music added later by his friend Daniel E. Kelley.

I Ride an Old Paint

A "paint" horse is a breed of western stock horse with a pinto spotting pattern of white and dark colors, and "Old Dan" would be a packhorse or a mule. A "hoolihan" is a style of loop used when throwing a rope, and a "coulee" is a small stream or dry stream bed.

I'm Happy

A poem by Waddie Mitchell set to music by Pipp Gillette.

It Could Have Been Worse

A poem by Waddie Mitchell set to music by Pipp Gillette, pretty much a list of Waddie's "wrecks" from his buckaroo days. A "latigo" is a long leather strap on a western saddle used to adjust the cinch.

Jack O' Diamonds

One of several traditional songs by this name, and with several verses also found in other similar songs. From the singing of Connie Dover, who spends her summers as a ranch cook in northwestern Wyoming and as a cook and guide at a remote winter camp in Yellowstone National Park.

Leaving Cheyenne

Also known as "Goodbye Old Paint". Jess Morris recorded it for John Lomax, and he had learned it from Charlie Willis who was an African-American cowboy on the XIT Ranch.

The Lily of the West

An old murder ballad that dates to at least 1842.

The Little Black Bull

There are many different variations of this song dating back to 1858 or before. This was "Teddy Blue" Abbott's favorite song in 1883.

Little Joe, the Wrangler

Written by Jack Thorp in 1898. A "wrangler" is the cowboy who takes care of the horses on a ranch or cattle drive, and a "remuda" is the group of saddle horses used by cowboys in herding cattle.

The Little Old Sod Shanty

Dating to at least the 1880's and derived from "The Little Old Log Cabin in the Lane" written by Will S. Hayes in 1871.

The Lone Star Trail

First published by John Lomax in 1910 and learned from "crippled-up, retired cowboy" Alec Moore.

Long Summer Day

Reported to be an old slave work song collected by John and Alan Lomax, with new cowboy lyrics by the Gillette Brothers.

Middle of Nowhere

A poem by Waddie Mitchell set to music by Pipp Gillette.

Mustang Gray

Mabry "Mustang" Gray was a bloodthirsty Texian who fought for Texas independence in the 1830's. This ballad dates to 1884.

The Night-Herding Song

Composed by cowboy Harry Stephens in 1909 while night-herding wild horses in Yellowstone National Park in Wyoming. Night-herding songs were vitally important for keeping the cowboy awake and the cattle asleep.

North to Kansas

Inspired by Ewan MacColl's "Shoals of Herring", Pipp & Guy Gillette wrote new lyrics about the toil and trouble of driving cattle to market in Kansas.

Ocean of Grass

Starting with the traditional sea song "The Mermaid", Guy Gillette wrote new lyrics about the threat of a cattle stampede.

Oh Bury Me Not on the Lone Prairie

Also known as "The Cowboy's Lament" and "The Dying Cowboy" this is one of the most famous cowboy songs and is adapted from the poem "The Ocean-Buried" by Reverend Edwin Hubbell Chapin published in 1839.

Oh My Darling Clementine

The words are based on the 1863 song "Down by the River Lived a Maiden" by H.S. Thompson, but the sheet music from 1884 credited to Percy Montrose contains the words and music that is known today.

Oh! Susanna

Perhaps the most famous song written by Stephen Foster (in 1848), this is the Gillette Brothers version.

The Old Chisholm Trail

Pronounced "chizzum", this song dates back to the 1870's and was first published by John Lomax in 1910 with over 70 verses.

Old Dan Tucker

The first song written by the king of the minstrel show writers, Dan Emmett, in 1843. Emmett is most famous for writing "Dixie".

The Overlanders

Australian stockmen and drovers were often called "overlanders" due to the long journeys driving their herds to market. From Warren Fahey's epic book of Australian Folksong *Eureka – The Songs that Made Australia*.

The Pot Wrastler

Written by old-time cowboy and cowboy poet Curley Fletcher. The word "buckaroo" derives from the Spanish "vaquero".

Puʻu Huluhulu

A paniolo (Hawaiian cowboy) song from the Big Island of Hawaii about spotting an unusual hill (puʻu) with trees on it that means you're almost home.

The Rambling Gambler

Collected by John Lomax from retired cowpuncher Alec Moore. Similar to "Rye Whiskey" and the old English folk song "Waggoner's Lad".

The Red River Valley

This song was most likely written in Canada as early at 1870 about the Red River Valley in Manitoba – and not about the Red River Valley between Oklahoma and Texas. Oddly enough, this song is hugely popular in China.

Red Wing

Written in 1907 as an "Indian Intermezzo" with words by Thurland Chattaway and music that Kerry Mills adapted from Robert Schumann's "The Happy Farmer". The original sheet music features a very colorful Indian maiden in full feathered headdress.

Roundup in the Spring

A traditional song of unknown authorship that collector J. Frank Dobie learned from a cowboy named Andy Adams.

Rye Whiskey

A song with many variations and floating verses, first published by Alan Lomax in 1910.

Sam Bass

Named for the 19th century Old West train robber and outlaw who died at age 27 in a gun battle with the Texas Rangers. The "U.P." train refers to the Union Pacific robbery that netted him $60,000 in 1877.

The Santa Fe Trail

Written in 1911 by James Grafton Rogers who would later become a famous diplomat, mountaineer, poet, educator, mayor, lawyer and Assistant Secretary of State in the Hoover administration.

Sentiment Toast

From a poem by Waddie Mitchell set to music by Pipp Gillette.

The Strawberry Roan

First published as a poem written in 1915 by cowboy Curley Fletcher. "Caballo" is the Spanish word for horse. To "fan" is to wave your hat while riding a bucking bronco.

The Streets of Laredo

Also known as the "Cowboy's Lament" this song started out as a traditional Irish song "The Unfortunate Rake". The New Orleans standard "St. James Infirmary" also derives from the same song. Cowboy and carpenter Frank Maynard claimed to have written the cowboy lyrics c.1876. In 1941 Burl Ives recorded it to the tune of "The Bard of Armagh" and that is the melody it is known by today.

Sweet Betsy From Pike

A song from the California Gold Rush with lyrics by writer-entertainer John A. Stone ("Old Put") published in 1858.

Ten Thousand Cattle Straying

Written by Owen Wister and first published in 1904 for a stage production of his famous novel, *The Virginian*.

The Texas Cowboy

Composed by Mrs Robt Thomson and published in Galveston in 1886, from the Lester S. Levy Sheet Music Collection at Johns Hopkins University. Her only other known composition is a Christmas song "Compliments of the Season" (1885).

Texian Boys

John Lomax learned this from J.D. Mitchell of Victoria, Texas, who learned it in 1868 from someone who said it dated back to the days of the Texas Republic.

The Trail to Mexico

First published by John Lomax in 1910, and possibly derived from "The Seaman's Complaint for his Unkind Mistress of Wapping" dating way back to the 1680's.

When the Morning Comes

Charles Albert Tindley was the son of a slave who became a very popular Methodist minister in Philadelphia who also wrote dozens of hymns. He wrote this one in 1905 with the chorus based on the traditional African-American spiritual "By an' By".

When the Work's All Done This Fall

Written by cowboy poet D.J. O'Malley in 1893 after his friend, Charlie Rutledge, was killed in a stampede.

Windy Bill

First published by Jack Thorp in 1908. A "Sam Stack Tree" was a type of carved wooden framework for a saddle, "maguey" (pronounced "mah-GAY") is a rope made from the Mexican agave or century plant, and "dally welter" is to wrap a rope around the saddle horn as opposed to tying on "hard and fast", from the Spanish "dale vuelta" which means to "give it a turn".

The Yellow Rose of Texas

First published in 1858 and attributed to "J.K.". This song was extremely popular throughout Texas and with the Southern troops in the American Civil War.

The Zebra Dun

This song was collected by Jack Thorp in 1890 from Randolph Reynolds at Carrizozo Flats in New Mexico. The "dun factor" is a genetic trait that tends to lighten the base coat of a horse, and it is often accompanied by striping.

RESOURCES

Cannon, Hal. *Old-Time Cowboy Songs.* Salt Lake City: Peregrine Smith Books, 1988

Fife, Austin E. and Alta S. *Cowboy and Western Songs.* New York: Clarkson N. Potter, Inc., 1969

Larkin, Margaret. *Singing Cowboy.* New York: Alfred Knopf Inc., 1931

Lomax, John A. & Alan. *Cowboy Songs and other Frontier Ballads.* New York: The Macmillan Company, 1941

Ohrlin, Glenn. *The Hell-Bound Train.* Texas Tech University Press, 2016

Thorp, N. Howard. *Songs of the Cowboys.* Boston, New York: Houghton Mifflin Company, 1908/1921

White, John. *Git Along Little Dogies.* University of Illinois Press, 1975

A TIP OF THE STETSON

Gene Autry
Hal Cannon
Wilf Carter
Connie Dover
Don Edwards
Elko National Cowboy Poetry Gathering
Guy & Pipp Gillette
Steve & Sheryl Hartz
Fran Hedrick
Jody Kruskal
Margaret Larkin
Alan Lomax
John A. Lomax
William Matthews
Waddie Mitchell
Michael Martin Murphey
Glenn Ohrlin
Buck Ramsey
Riders in the Sky
Marty Robbins
Roy Rogers
Sons of the Pioneers
Clyde "Kindy" Sproat
Jack Thorp
John White
Bernard Wrigley

THE AUTHORS

Gary Coover

Growing up in Oklahoma, Gary heard cowboy songs at an early age, first rode a horse at the age of five, and as a small child loved to go out into the countryside and "moo at the cows". Not sure how they felt about it, but at least at the time he thought it was something important to do!

Fast forward to college years in Houston, Texas, summer jobs in West Texas and New Mexico, and many years as producer and host of the "Shepherd's Hey" radio program featuring traditional music of the British Isles and Ireland. While performing on the concertina at the Texas Folklife Festival in San Antonio he met and became lifelong friends with oldtime musician Steve Hartz, and through Steve he met Pipp and Guy Gillette one hot East Texas night when they were both most excellent performers and shills at a performance of the Atoyac Valley Medicine Show.

Gary has published several books for the Anglo concertina, including two books of sea shanties and a collection of songs and tunes from the American Civil War. Lucky for him, his work and travels have taken him through every state in the Great American West.

Pipp Gillette

An award-winning cowboy singer and chuckwagon aficionado, Pipp raises cattle on the family ranch near Lovelady, Texas, that his grandfather started in 1912. He plays traditional cowboy music on guitar, banjo, harmonica and bones, and writes songs and sets cowboy poetry to music.

Pipp and his late brother Guy Gillette recorded eight albums of cowboy music and were recipients of the Western Heritage Wrangler Award for Best Traditional Album of 2010 for their CD "Cowboys, Minstrels and Medicine Shows". The Gillette Brothers were recipients of the 2009 American Cowboy Culture Award for western music from the National Cowboy Symposium & Celebration. They were awarded the 2003 and the 1998 Will Rogers Award for Outstanding Achievement in the Advancement of Contemporary Cowboy Music Best Duo/Group by The Academy of Western Artists. And they have also received the National Cowboy Symposium's American Cowboy Culture Chuck Wagon Award.

In 2016 Pipp was the winner of the Western Heritage Award for "Traditional Western Album" from the National Cowboy & Western Heritage Museum in Oklahoma City for the album "Singing Songs by Waddie & Pipp".

Pipp has performed at cowboy poetry gatherings and festivals throughout the US, including the 2008 Smithsonian Folklife Festival in Washington DC, the National Cowboy Poetry Gathering in Elko, NV, the Monterey Cowboy Poetry & Music Festival in Monterey, CA, the Santa Clarita Cowboy Poetry & Music Festival in Santa Clarita, CA, the International Storytelling Festival in Jonesborough, TN, the Willow Tree Festival in Gordon, NE, the Arizona Cowboy Poets Gathering in Prescott, AZ, the Buffalo Bill Historical Center in Cody, WY, the National Cowboy Symposium Lubbock, TX, the Texas Cowboy Poetry Gathering in Alpine, TX, and the National Cowboy & Western Heritage Museum in Oklahoma City, OK.

GILLETTE BROTHERS RECORDINGS

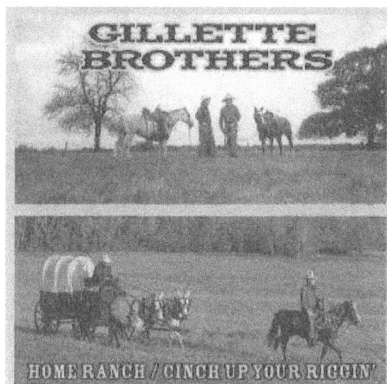

Home Ranch (1992)
Cinch Up Your Riggin' (1994)

Lone Star Trail (1997)

Live from the Camp Street Café
& Store (2001)

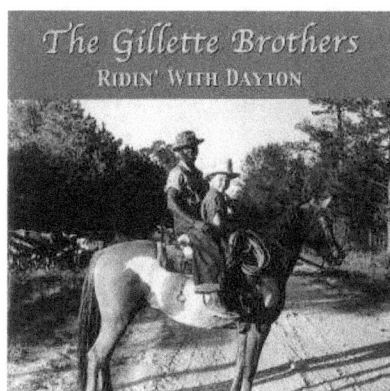

Ridin' With Dayton (2003)

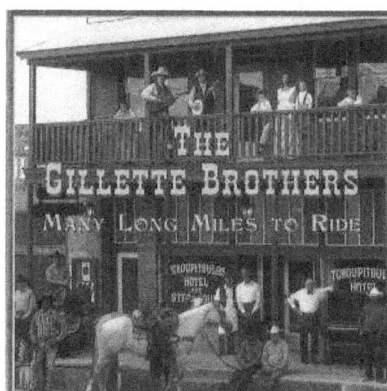

Many Long Miles to Ride (2006)

Cowboys, Minstrels and
Medicine Shows (2010)

Leaving Cheyenne (2012)

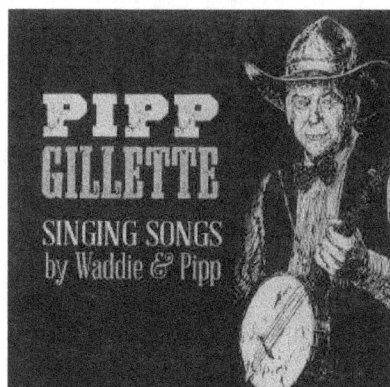

Singing Songs by Waddie & Pipp
(2015)

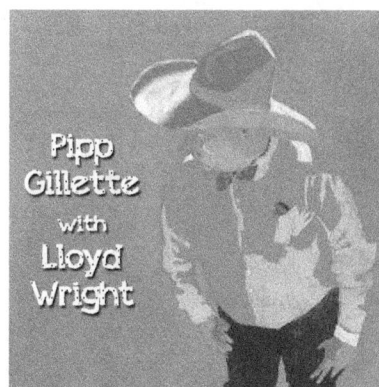

Pipp Gillette with
Lloyd Wright (2018)

CD's available from the Camp St. Café & Store
215 S. 3rd Street, Crockett, Texas 75835
www.campstreetcafe.com

NATIONAL COWBOY POETRY GATHERING

Photo by Charlie Ekburg

Since 1985, The National Cowboy Poetry Gathering in Elko, Nevada, has been *the* place where Western ranchers and cowboys could gather to share poems and tell their stories of hard work, heartbreak and hilarity, and what it means to make your way in the rangeland.

Athough there are now many gatherings of Western poets, musicians, artisans and storytellers across the country – the Elko Gathering was where it all started.

Known simply as "Elko" to many, the Gathering embraces its role as a pilgrimage destination for thousands of ranch folk and others who love the West and come to learn and experience art that grows from a connection to the rhythms of earth and sky.

Organized by the Western Folklife Center, The National Cowboy Poetry Gathering is six days of poetry, music, dancing, workshops, exhibits, conversations, food and fellowship, rooted in tradition but focused on today's rural West. It has become an annual ritual for thousands of people who value and practice the artistic traditions of the region and are concerned about the present and future of the West.

Photo by Sydney Martinez/TravelNevada

Held during the last week in January each year, the Gathering has grown from the 60 chairs set out by Western Folklife Center founding director Hal Cannon and poet Waddie Mitchell to over 8,000 attendees and performers, and now features 40+ poets, musicians, and storytellers across five different stages.

Photo by Sydney Martinez/TravelNevada

The Gathering also includes workshops, film screenings, open mics, and educational programming. Ranchfolk, rural denizens and enthusiasts of the American West are captivated by poets and musicians whose verses speak of a life lived on the land. They listen, they learn, they kick up their heels and enjoy a week filled with entertainment, delight and laughter.

Cowboys from around the world have been brought in to share their traditions, celebrating ranching culture everywhere from Mongolia to the Basque county, Canada to Argentina, and most of all the American West. Poets, storytellers, singers, guitar players, banjo players, fiddlers, and squeezebox players are all welcome to come share their cowboy stories and Western experiences.

www.nationalcowboypoetrygathering.org

Cowboy Songs Old & New